Rethinking Teacher Education

Rethinking Teacher Education

A Bold Alternative to Preservice Programs

Selma Wassermann

ROWMAN & LITTLEFIELD
Lanham • Boulder • New York • London

Published by Rowman & Littlefield
An imprint of The Rowman & Littlefield Publishing Group, Inc.
4501 Forbes Boulevard, Suite 200, Lanham, Maryland 20706
www.rowman.com

86-90 Paul Street, London EC2A 4NE, United Kingdom

Copyright © 2022 by Selma Wassermann

All rights reserved. No part of this book may be reproduced in any form or by any electronic or mechanical means, including information storage and retrieval systems, without written permission from the publisher, except by a reviewer who may quote passages in a review.

British Library Cataloguing in Publication Information Available

Library of Congress Cataloging-in-Publication Data

ISBN: 978-1-4758-6335-2 (cloth)
ISBN: 978-1-4758-6336-9 (pbk.)
ISBN: 978-1-4758-6337-6 (electronic)

Contents

Preface: The Harpsichord Theory of Teacher Education . . . vii

Acknowledgments . . . xi

Introduction . . . xiii

Chapter 1: Where Do We Start? . . . 1

Chapter 2: Connecting Means with Ends . . . 9

Chapter 3: To Know, to Understand, and to Know How: A Theoretical Framework . . . 19

Chapter 4: Some Radical Ideas . . . 33

PART II: DEVELOPING COMPETENCE . . . 41

Chapter 5: Introduction to Part II . . . 43

Chapter 6: Developing Competence: Kids—Learning to Observe, Diagnose, and Deal with Individual Behavior . . . 45

Chapter 7: Developing Competence: Teacher-Student Interactions . . . 53

Chapter 8: Developing Competence: The Teacher as Curriculum Maker . . . 65

Chapter 9: Developing Competence: Student Teaching . . . 75

Chapter 10: In Retrospect . . . 85

Appendix . . . 89

Bibliography . . . 93

Index	95
About the Author	101

Preface

The Harpsichord Theory of Teacher Education

GETTING ADMITTED

The day was cold and rainy when I reached his office, and all of the preparations I had made to look neat and presentable had fallen by the wayside during my walk from the subway station to the education building. He offered me a chair without looking up and I sat, tugged at my wet jacket, and waited.

"So why do you want to be a teacher?" he asked without smiling. This was to be the interview that could allow me to enter the teacher education program at the City University. I was excited, nervous, and a sleepless night of anxiety didn't help me to calm down. I gave him the standard reply: "I like children."

"So why don't you get married and have some?" There was a bit of deadness in his response, and I didn't know what to say next. The silence between us filled the space and hung there. He wrote something down on sheets of paper and inserted the sheets into a folder, placing it on a pile at the edge of his desk. He then looked up at me and said, "You are too overweight for the program."

His remark stunned me. I was hardly obese, but certainly not thin. I told him that I would go on a diet and lose 10 pounds before the term began. Would I then qualify?

His pen tapped on the edge of the folder and without further word, he dismissed me. On my way back to the subway I stopped at a Starbucks and bought a café latte and a donut, certain that I had failed to meet his standards of admission into the teacher education program.

When the letter came announcing that I had been accepted, I was mystified. By what criteria had he made his judgment? What did I say that met his standards? How did my weight have anything to do with it? Or was that interview just another one of the incomprehensible hurdles that I would face in becoming a teacher?

TRAINING PROGRAM

The course was titled Methods and Materials of Teaching, three credits, and Professor Melvin stood at the front of the classroom with the authority of his several degrees behind him, as we students sat, watched, and listened to him describe what constituted "good teaching." He admonished us to be mindful of individual learning differences. We were to be "on top" of curriculum requirements issued by school and state boards of education; to know about children presenting learning difficulties and how to deal with them; to understand how to maintain classroom control and how to deal with behavioral problems. We needed to be knowledgeable about how IT could be used to enrich curriculum activities.

The list of "shoulds" was formidable, and we copied them assiduously into our notebooks or laptops ready to recall and reframe them for the final exam. The course was one of the requirements that led to a bachelor of education degree that would qualify us to become certified teachers in the state of New York. In the 36 hours of required coursework, not a single course deviated from the same model: teacher-centered lectures and a long list of "to dos" that would enable us to face the 30-odd children in our own classrooms, with not only competence but panache.

From time to time, we were given assignments generating lesson plans in the abstract, without any consideration of the makeup of an actual class, and research projects that had as little to do with classroom life as chalk to cheese.

Little wonder, then, that upon facing that first class of a mixed bunch of third graders, I fumbled and stumbled and mumbled my way through the day, barely able to recall the many "shoulds" and unhappily unable to find the means to put them into practice, a testament to the most frequently heard criticisms of teacher education: the yawning abyss between telling preservice students in education how they should teach, and providing them with meaningful opportunities to translate the "shoulds" into classroom applications.

Although a small part of this deficit is met during the student teaching semester, for most students, that experience comes too little, too late and depends very much on the competence and willingness of the practicum teacher to take on the additional burden of seeing to the developing expertise of the student teacher.

In the years that followed, I found, to my astonishment and consternation, that what I had endured during my preservice preparation and my first days of teaching was not unique. It was the same for very many of us entering the classroom for the first time: a universally shared trauma. The ordeal of those first 60 days are the beginning teacher's initiation rites into the profession, the time during which we face up to the bankruptcy of what little we know about teaching. It is the time during which we begin to teach ourselves how to survive in the classroom.

Some of us teach ourselves to teach in the process. It is either that or making cabbage rolls, in the kitchen or in the classroom.

WHAT'S WRONG WITH THIS PICTURE?

What is it, exactly, that is missing from our training programs? Why do beginning teachers feel disabled, rather than enabled, during those first critical weeks of teaching?

Besides the spurious admission criteria, imagine, for a moment, a scenario in which a student wished to learn to play the harpsichord. Imagine her attending university classes for four years, during which she engaged primarily in listening to her teachers play their harpsichords, and which culminated in a practicum experience of actual harpsichord playing lasting only five months. It would be beyond silly to expect this student to perform as a competent professional. We are content that she has learned to play "The Happy Farmer." Her technical skills are understandably weak and her artistry nonexistent. We would not dream of awarding her a certificate so that she might now teach others.

Yet this is the route by which students are expected to learn how to become classroom teachers. It is no wonder that so many graduate lacking both the technical skills and the artistry. Little wonder that so many who choose to remain in the profession fall back on what they know best: emulating their own classroom teachers, in grades 1 through 12. Little wonder that so many opt out. What, then, were all those 36 credits of education classes all about?

In the 50 years since my teacher education days at the City University, the program offered for teacher preparation is largely the same. Yes, the names of the courses are somewhat different; yes, the old teachers have retired and been replaced by new ones; yes, some of the courses recognize more current issues like "Education of the Gifted" and "Students with Disabilities," but the manner of presentation is the same. In the most important sense, nothing has changed to address the huge disconnect between "means" and "ends."

Acknowledgments

Much of the material included in this text comes from my work with my preservice students preparing to enter the teaching profession. It is to them that I owe the greatest debt; it is due to their dedication, their help, their compassion, their earnest desire to become good teachers, that I have learned much about effective practices in teacher education. They have been my very best teachers and it has been my privilege to know them, to teach them, and to see them now as colleagues.

Simon Fraser University has provided me with the "growing ground" in which I was able to put new ideas into practice, to learn from those field trials, and to make necessary changes in what I was attempting to do. It is rare that a university faculty offers such flexibility and the options for making changes. It was that fertile soil in which I was able to move forward in my understanding and implementation of connecting my teaching practices to my goals.

On the home front I have been aided and abetted in my writing by my family; Paula, my fount of wisdom for keeping me grounded and focused; Simon, the wizard of Parksville, who addresses, with compassion, every computer urgency; Arlo, whose life is a lodestar in pointing to what lies outside of my workspace; and my three adorables, Maya, Kai, and Ruben, who light up my life and keep me in touch with what it is like to be a child in school.

To my publisher, Tom Koerner, who gives me license to keep writing; to my editors at Rowman & Littlefield; to Teachers College Press and Anne Bauer at Childhood Education for their permission to adapt material from previously published articles and books; and finally to those colleagues who have so generously agreed to read and endorse the work of this book, Gary Squire, George Ivany, Tom O'Shea, Wally Eggert, and Bill Cliett, my warmest thanks.

Introduction

The chair of the secondary education faculty at a leading midwestern university had called this special meeting to hear the report of the committee that had spent two years gathering data from students and faculty to assess the current secondary teacher education program and make recommendations for improvement. The group of 24 professors sipped coffee, dunked biscuits, and wiped crumbs from their laps, while listening to the reports of their colleagues. The news was not affirming.

Students reported that the courses that had been required to complete their training were, by and large, ineffectual. Many of them complained that their coursework did not prepare them for the real life of the classroom. Several faculty members pointed to how the structure of the faculty itself militated against change. The committee made some clear and helpful recommendations for how the program might be improved, from more careful and studied admissions of students to the methods used in the various courses, as well as to extending the length of the student teaching practicum.

At the close of the report, a hush fell. The chair thanked the committee for their report and for the work they did gathering the data that contributed to their findings. More silence.

The chair then queried, "What chances, do you suppose, would there be for initiating some of the recommendations of the committee to make the necessary changes to the program?" There was a shuffling of feet, some tittering, and then, "None at all."

The chair closed the pages of the report, thanked the group for their attendance, and watched as his colleagues filed out of the meeting room.

WHAT'S WRONG WITH TEACHER EDUCATION?

Authors Zeichner (2018) and Levine (2006) have studied teacher education programs and both have written about the inadequacies of teacher preparation. "By almost any standard, many, if not most, of the nation's 1,450 schools, colleges, and departments of education are doing a mediocre job of preparing teachers" (Zeichner, 2018).

Levine's (2006) comprehensive study of graduates of teacher education programs reported that despite a few "model" teacher education programs,[1] the majority of teachers are prepared in programs that have low admission and graduation standards, "clinging to an outdated, historically flawed vision of teacher education, resulting in many graduating without the skills and knowledge they need to become effective teachers."

"Of all the hours I was at graduate school, I don't think there was all together an hour devoted to classroom management. We were developing beautifully crafted lesson plans that no one could use. I was learning esoteric phrases about test design. I spent two semesters doing a research project. I just wish somebody had told me how to get a cellphone out of a kid's hands" (Leland, 2016).

There are many reasons for this, reasons that make such programs resistant to change. In many colleges and universities, education is one of the "cash cows" of the institution, with low admission standards that make it possible for their large enrollments to support financially those other programs that are in budgetary shortfall. More than a few professors who come to teach in these programs are themselves without experience as teachers in public schools and are more preoccupied with their own tenure and promotion aspects than they are about the practice of teaching. Very few have a clear idea of how to design a course that emphasizes how to connect the ideas they are promoting with the realities of classroom life.

Perhaps the most compelling argument against change is that there is no incentive to improve teaching. At the college and university levels of instruction, the important "rewards" are given for publications in learned journals and mega dollar grants that fund research. What they do in their courses has little or nothing to do with how professors earn what's important: tenure and promotion.

In the brief scenario cited above, there was no incentive for professors, steeped in their own traditional roles and happily and safely secured in their tenure, to change. The impetus to change must arise from a clearly articulated need. If one is safely ensconced in what he or she is doing, the urgency for change simply does not exist. Living an "examined life" as a teacher is not a requirement for advancement in schools of education.

The aims of this book include some concrete and specific suggestions for how teacher education programs might be re-created, beginning with the need to identify and connect means with goals, identifying key ingredients for pre-service preparation, structuring the shape of a program to allow for the kinds of skill development necessary for new teachers, and providing tools for more effective evaluation of teaching practice.

Suggestions are also made for different methods of implementation. Forsaking a total upheaval of existing programs, some ideas are included for how a few interested and dedicated professors of education may develop "mini schools" within existing programs that can better ensure that means are consistent with the goals.

The ideas in this book do not come from the author's invention but reflect existing programs that have proven to be effective over the years in providing new teachers with the skills, the understandings, and the teaching strategies necessary for success. The author, one of the pioneers of the successful and highly acclaimed Professional Development Program at Simon Fraser University, draws on her own experiences with the shaping and the evolving of the program to provide details, and specifics to encourage and help others to find their way to the much-needed improvements for change—those that offer the best opportunities for new teachers to face and tackle the many challenges of today's classrooms.

Chapter 1, "Where Do We Start?" begins with how to make means consistent with ends in teacher preparation and includes a reexamination of criteria for admission to teacher education programs.

Chapter 2, "Connecting Means with Ends," identifies some key ingredients in teacher preparation and focuses on essential skills a new teacher needs.

Chapter 3, "To Know, to Understand, and to Know How," presents a theoretical framework that may be used to design more effective teaching methods.

Chapter 4, "Some Radical Ideas," offers some innovative ideas for modifying existing programs.

Chapter 5, "Introduction to Part II," introduces the next four chapters, which deal with the development of competence in specific teaching areas.

Chapter 6, "Developing Competence: Kids—Learning to Observe, Diagnose, and Deal with Individual Behavior," suggests ways in which students may learn to deal more effectively with children's presenting behaviors.

Chapter 7, "Developing Competence: Teacher-Student Interactions," includes developing students' competence in using effective interactive strategies that promote children's thoughtful inquiry into the "big ideas."

Chapter 8, "Developing Competence: The Teacher as Curriculum Maker," provides tools for understanding and developing relevant curriculum experiences.

Chapter 9, "Developing Competence: Student Teaching," offers suggestions for how to make the most of student teaching experiences.

Chapter 10, "In Retrospect," is a summary of the key principles that can be extracted from the proposals in this book.

NOTE

1. Alverno College, Bank Street College of Education, High Tech High's Intern Program, Montclair State University, San Francisco Teacher Residency, Trinity University, and University of Colorado Denver.

Chapter 1

Where Do We Start?

The obvious starting point in rethinking teacher education is to reconsider how students are admitted to professional programs. In many schools of education, the single criterion is grade point average. No one would dispute that good grades indicate a certain level of intelligence that would be a requirement for anyone wishing to play a role in educating the young. Yet grades, in and of themselves, do not reveal some other important attributes in a prospective candidate that bear in important ways on a teacher's effectiveness and on student learning.

There are, alas, no hard and fast characteristics that are guarantees of future professional competence in a candidate. Some teachers begin weakly, but happily develop expertise on the job over the years. Some come into the profession with advanced skills, and even as newcomers show professional competence that belies their lack of experience on the job. These are not anomalies, but rather point to the "iffiness" of making reliable and sound judgments at the point of entry.

Given the fact that judgments at entry point are fallible, that judgments lie in the eyes of the beholders, and that grades are insufficient as evidence of the promise of professional competence, what then might be some attributes or characteristics that applicants to a teacher education program might reveal initially that would make them more eligible? What data should faculty be looking for in a candidate's application?

The characteristics that follow may not provide a "lock" between the attributes and "teaching promise," but at the very least, they implicitly point to more effective and more satisfying human relationships—the litmus test of how teachers connect with students. "Education watchers have long known that the relationship with a teacher can be critically important to how well students learn" (Sparks, 2019). The examination of such positive attributes in candidates' applications would be one starting point in admissions.

SOME IMPORTANT CHARACTERISTICS

No one expects new teachers to shine with expertise on their first days, weeks, even months in the classroom. But there may be certain attributes that can be identified, at the point of admission, that suggest fertile ground for teacher effectiveness. What follows are some recommendations of what to look for in a candidate's application—those attributes that would appear to allow for more effective relationships with students.

It will be quickly discerned that the recommendations fall into the category of "human relationship" characteristics. They are the attributes that are identified as necessary in most human relationship professions. For as Arthur Combs and others reminded us, "it's the relationship that teaches more than the subject" (Combs & Gonzales, 1993; Henschke, 2013).

a. Genuineness

Sometimes it's called authenticity. Sometimes congruence. Sometimes genuineness. These descriptors refer to a person's ability to be "real." Many authors who write about human relationships (e.g., Carkhuff, 1969; Greenberg and Johnson, 1978; Moustakas, 1966; Rogers, 1961) claim that genuineness is the most important attribute in effective human relationships.

At the opposite end of the genuineness continuum is phoniness—the donning of a professional facade behind which to hide one's real self. It is the attribute that even young children are especially sensitive to; they will tell you in no uncertain terms that their teacher's phoniness is off-putting.

In the literature on human relationships, it has been not only suggested but documented that persons in the helping professions are more likely to be effective when they are genuine, less effective if they are phony (Truax and Mitchell, 1971). That is why this attribute stands at the head of the list of what to look for in a candidate's application to a teacher education program. This is probably the least "trainable" attribute in a prospective teacher.

b. Respect

In a close second to "genuineness" is the attribute of being respectful—showing respect for the children in one's care, no matter how young. To communicate respect for children is to give them opportunities to make choices for themselves—to treat them as one would other adults, courteously and with full regard. This includes being considerate of their feelings and of their ideas. It also includes allowing them more degrees of freedom to decide for themselves about matters of consequence in their classroom routines.

This attribute is as important in working with young children as it is for those older students, even though freedom to choose for the younger groups may be considerably more limited.

Respect is absent when teachers are overly critical; when they give unasked-for advice; when they believe they always know better what is right and good for a child, or for a group; when they show little regard for the feelings and ideas of individuals or of the group.

Respect is a mainstay in all effective human relationships and is seen in classrooms where teacher and children really like each other; where children enjoy coming to class. When respect is clearly present in a teacher's relationships with students, a climate of safety and of care is created and is a significant part of the learning ethos.

c. Non-defensiveness

Another strong attribute is a candidate's non-defensiveness in owning up to their shortcomings. This is easier said than done; very few of us are willing or able to risk showing our imperfections. We have learned over time to hide any imperfections behind a facade of protective defensiveness. To a child who says, "Ms. Blake, you told us we didn't need to study those math problems, but they were on the test anyway," the tempting response is to reproach, to defend one's position by explaining the reasons for the action.

It is much harder to put yourself in the child's place and appreciate his point of view.

An open, non-defensive response might offer:

"I know I said that and I'm sorry that I misled you. I should have remembered that they were important, and I should have told you that. I apologize."

When teachers can respond to their students non-defensively, when they can be more open about their own feelings and tune in to the feelings their students are expressing, the impact on teacher-student relationships is powerfully additive. Such an attribute contributes substantially to the quality of human relationships and makes life in classrooms that much more agreeable.

d. Non-dogmatism

It is probably true that one of the most reductive characteristics in a classroom discourse is a teacher's dogmatism. If a teacher believes, truly and deeply, that he or she has all the answers, knows all the facts, knows without equivocation the reasons that explain certain situations, there is no room for further examination. A student who wants to offer another idea, another opinion, an alternate point of view, is often put down. This teacher has no reason to doubt, no reason to consider a different version of events. A teacher's dogmatism is probably the most virulent attribute in stifling student thinking.

At the opposite end of dogmatism is the candidate who is open to examining new ideas, who is comfortable with dissonance, who can suspend judgment when the data are inconclusive. This is the candidate who is more likely to be able to offer students greater opportunities to think, to invent, to come up with ideas that go beyond the obvious, that lead to new and more creative applications.

At entry point, evidence that a candidate is certain, where there is room for doubt; who is definite, when there is an absence of data; who is opinionated when he or she should be circumspect may be someone who is the least prepared to offer students a chance to have their own ideas, to open their minds, to examine critically, to think.

e. Dependency

A candidate who reveals his or her dependency in the extreme may be the least likely to be able to grow professionally on the job. These are people who look to others for advice, for guidance, for help in moving forward. They need to be told what to do. They are unable or afraid to act on their own.

These candidates may more than likely turn into teachers who never veer from the standard routines; they teach in the same old same old ways. Their lesson plans are yellowed with age, and their routines never vary. The students say the classes are boring and lifeless. New ideas, new ways, innovations are threatening to these teachers.

At the opposite end of this continuum is the candidate who reveals a strong sense of independence in being able to take the initiative, who is unafraid to try something new, who is able to look at errors in judgment or action, examine what went wrong, and try again.

A case could be made that the above attributes have little or nothing to do with students' performance on standardized tests. While that may be the case, there is surely more to teaching and learning than is revealed on test performance. There is a climate in a classroom that is created by how a teacher behaves that contributes, in a large measure, to student affect—the climate that makes it more comfortable for students to learn. It is what the teacher "models" in the classroom that communicates the ways in which we hope people behave toward each other.

To argue the case further, it is more likely that students would be more comfortable and therefore more responsive working in a classroom where a teacher exhibited such positive attributes than in a classroom where they were absent or seen in their opposites.

SOME STRATEGIES FOR DISCERNING HUMAN RELATIONSHIPS ATTRIBUTES IN APPLICANTS

It would be so easy if we could administer a DNA test to see if these "human relationship" attributes were present in a potential candidate for a teacher education program. It would be so easy if we could administer a true/false test to determine whether a candidate was genuine, or non-defensive, or non-dogmatic. Alas, there are no easy routes or shortcuts to make such determinations. The best strategies lie in the way those on the admissions committee "read into" and make interpretations of what a candidate is presenting in application documents that are designed to allow for disclosure of those attributes.

Such qualitative assessments are fallible of course—but within them lie the promise of at least making clear what a faculty considers important in a candidate. Within them lie the potential of finding whether such characteristics exist in the applications. The good news is that such assessments are not life-and-death judgments. Erring on the side of caution and allowing a candidate entry may not be an accurate assessment. But nothing is lost. There will be many subsequent opportunities to discern whether, during coursework or the student teaching practicum, that candidate does, in fact, have the "right stuff" to make a difference in the lives of students and whether there is the promise of continued self-reflection and ongoing professional growth.

These qualitative assessments are correlate with the first criterion for acceptance: a student's grade point average. This is because no one wants a teacher to be illiterate; to not be able to write a clear sentence; to not be able to spell; to be unknowledgeable about history, geography, current events, economics, mathematics, and good literature. It may be helpful to remember that while qualitative assessments are fallible, so are grades as indicators of whether a candidate will be a successful teacher.

SEARCHING FOR EVIDENCE IN PORTFOLIOS

Candidates wishing to be considered for a teacher education program should, at the outset, provide the admissions committee with a portfolio containing information that would reveal more about whether the "human relationships" attributes are to be found in the candidate's documentation. Candidates should be required to submit at least, some of the following:

a. Written evidence of volunteer work they have done with groups of children. This documentation may be personally related and/or provided by

an adult who supervised the candidate's work. Documentation from the children should also be included.
  b. A short video recording of the candidate's volunteer work with these or other groups of children.
  c. A personal statement indicating what the candidate believes are some of his or her important goals in teaching children.
  d. A brief autobiography that highlights some significant events in the candidate's life.
  e. Letters of reference from significant others such as former teachers.

This kind of documentation will reveal more about how the candidate behaves in interpersonal situations and should provide evidence of the existence, or lack of existence, of many, if not all, of these key human relationship attributes.

A helpful tool in assessing the documents would be to create a "rating scale" that would indicate the extent to which such attributes are in evidence—that is, is the evidence very clear, or seen somewhat, or not at all? Or are the attributes seen in negative views? This is probably more useful than an assessment in either/or terms.

SEARCHING FOR EVIDENCE IN CASE STUDIES

Another way of making determinations of candidates' human relationship attributes is to ask them to respond to a case study about a particular student or a teacher in a particular situation. The candidate's responses to a series of questions about the case should reveal a great deal about how the applicant sees children and/or teachers and their views on the goals of education in general.

An example of such a case is included in the appendix—but there are many others that are available in the literature about case method teaching. (See, for example, Kleinfeld, 1989; Greenwood and Parkay, 1989; Kowalski, Weaver, & Henson, 1990; Lloyd-Jones, 1956; Silverman et al., 1992; Wassermann, 1993.)

Candidates' responses to study questions that accompany the case should give insight into how they perceive the issues in the case, where they stand with respect to those issues, and what they see as some potential responses to this particular dilemma. The responses should yield a clearer picture of an applicant's human relationships attributes in the ways they respond to the issues in the case.

Once the admissions committee chooses to use portfolios and cases to reveal a candidate's human-relations characteristics, it would be important to vary cases used at each selection point; using the same case over the years will not only become tired but also lead prospective candidates to "tune in" to the kinds of responses that are more acceptable. In other words, they will quickly learn to "game the system." There is no dearth of fresh cases that can be rotated over time.

NOTES

Armed with not only GPA, but also documentation designed to reveal a candidate's human relationship attributes will give an admissions committee not only more data, but also more relevant data on which an informed decision can be made about a prospective candidate's eligibility to become a teacher. Yes, all human judgments are fallible; in the worst-case scenario a student will be admitted who proves unreliable or unpromising. If so, there will be recourse to reexamine the candidate's qualifications later in the program.

Chapter 2

Connecting Means with Ends

When Archie MacKinnon was appointed to become the first dean of the faculty of education at the very newly formed Simon Fraser University, tasked with the job of developing an innovative teacher education program, he began with two provocative questions:

What did we hope teachers would become as a result of spending a year in a professional program?

What were our views of "good teaching?"

At first glance such questions do not seem unusual or innovative; a beginning point for all program development would normally start with the identification of goals. Once the goals have been identified, the proposed means of reaching those goals become clearer. Nothing unusual about that.

Yet in most teacher education programs existing today, it is a rare occurrence that goals are identified in advance of the program development that follows. More likely, it is the inclusion of courses that comes first—adding those courses that are seen as necessary to prepare new teachers for facing the demands and challenges of today's classrooms. It is rare that a program is structured first, around the identification of those goals related to the important characteristics of teacher behavior, to be followed by coursework that closely articulates with the attainment of such goals.

What is largely missing from program planning and program design is the connection between means and ends. Teacher education programs that continue to use outdated and historically ineffective means have not, in the larger sense, sat down to consider first: what are the important goals we have for preparing new teachers to face the challenging and rigorous demands of today's classrooms; and second, if such be the goals, what are the best methods we can devise for attaining them?

It is a mystery why this is so uncommon, when the logic of such an approach is so clearly manifest.

As long ago as 1965, Combs (1965) wrote a comprehensive review of teacher education programs, citing the many criticisms that faulted them for being inadequate in design and methodology in the preparation of teachers. He concluded that "the product of all this discussion has so far been bitterly disappointing. For the most part it has resulted in little more than a reshuffling of the same old courses, a heavier load of content for teacher education students and some changes in procedures for certification and licensing." Fifty years later, in an article in the *Washington Post*, Mike Rose, from the faculty at the UCLA Graduate School of Education is quoted as saying, "Teacher education is a disaster" (Strauss, 2014).

Combs began his book with his identification of good teaching, "for whatever we do in teacher education must depend on our having some idea of the nature of good teaching—for to plan effective programs we need the very best definitions of good teaching we can get" (Combs, 1965).

GOALS OF TEACHER EDUCATION

As there are many roads that lead to Rome, there are also many concepts of "good teaching." In early days, the impression was that a good teacher needed to be a good scholar; it was assumed that a person who knew could teach. But of course, this notion failed in delivery because it is common knowledge that just "knowing" is not enough. As Combs has written, "most of us can recall, out of our own experiences, the teacher who knew his subject but couldn't put it across" (Combs, 1965).

In the history of the preparation of teachers, academics and researchers have developed lists that attempt to identify "specific competencies" of good teaching. From one such group, the list was exhaustive and not useful; for example (Combs, 1965):

Knows his subject
Knows much about related subjects
Is adaptable to new knowledge
Is able to recognize individual differences
Is a good communicator
Has an inquiring mind
Is available
Is committed
Is enthusiastic
Has a sense of humor
Has humility
Cherishes his [*sic*] own individuality
Has convictions
Is sincere and honest

Acts with integrity
Shows tolerance and understanding
Is caring
Has compassion
Has courage
Has personal security
Is creative
Is versatile
Is willing to try
Is adaptable
Believes in God

Raths (1964) articulated his own views of what a good teacher should be/do in his article about good teaching. He included the following characteristics:

Should be able to be clear in explaining, informing, and showing how
Should be self-initiating
Should be able to unify the group
Should be able to make the students feel secure
Should be able to clarify students' ideas, attitudes, problems
Should be able to diagnose students' learning problems
Should be able to create curriculum materials
Should be able to evaluate students' work intelligently and without being punitive
Should be able to organize and arrange the class for instructional purposes
Should be an active participant in professional and civic life

At about the same time, N. L. Gage offered his views of what he considered to be desirable behavioral characteristics of teachers of special needs students. These included warmth, cognitive organization, orderliness, indirectness, and the ability to solve instructional problems. He concluded his essay with the following comments: "Results thus far seem adequate to support the altogether plausible proposition that good teachers possess ability to solve technical problems in instruction. Apart from the social-emotional aspects of teaching behavior, the more strictly cognitive-intellectual ones, and the managerial phases of their work, good teachers need a unique body of problem-solving skills" (Gage, 1966).

A survey of the literature shows no dearth of ideas and opinions and even research findings that point to desirable characteristics of teaching behavior.

There are no clear answers as to why such behavioral characteristics, found in abundance in the literature on "what good teachers do" fail to lead to improvements in teacher education programs that would correlate with such goals. One hypothesis may relate to the lack of clarity of those goals. How, for example, would a course enable the development of Gage's idea of "warmth?" Or "cognitive organization?" Or "indirectness?"

As Combs (1965) suggested, perhaps the identification of behavioral characteristics as "good" or "desirable" is much too simple because the characteristics necessary for "good teaching" are likely to vary in different schools, with different sets of students, with different educational aims. However, all not is lost.

Applying the concept of "self as instrument" of the professional worker to teaching, it suggests that a teacher-education program must concern itself with the development of persons—the "production of creative individuals, capable of shifting and changing to meet the demands and opportunities afforded in daily tasks" (Combs, 1965).

Such a teacher would not behave in a pre-programmed way; the behavior will change from moment to moment, from day to day, adjusting continuously and smoothly to the needs of students, in the various and different situations, to the purposes and goals of the class and of the students, and the methods and materials on hand.

"The effective teacher is a unique human being who has learned to use himself [sic] effectively and efficiently to carry out his own and society's purposes in the education of others" (Combs, 1965).

Or as Maya, age ten, and Kai, age seven, put it when asked what they thought good teachers should be like: "Be kind and not yell at you when you make a mistake," and "Make more weekends."

How are such ideals then to be realized?

THE DEVELOPMENT OF A COMPETENCY-BASED PERFORMANCE INDEX

It won't come as news to anyone studying the history of teacher education that the well-intentioned lists of competences drafted by learned members of the academy have resulted in little significant change in the structures or processes of teacher training. Perhaps, like other changes of major consequence, the approach to change must come not from a revolution, but from a series of small but consequential steps toward making improvements—not in a massive overhaul, but by chipping away, piece by small piece, until a new "whole" is formed.

A few years after the initiation of the innovative Professional Development Program at Simon Fraser University, Wassermann & Eggert (1976) undertook a four-year study that led to the development of an assessment tool to identify important professional competencies in the training of student teachers. "For a competency instrument to work effectively," they wrote, "it must meet at least seven criteria":

1. It must assess the performance of the person in the context of the classroom. (That is, in examining a surgeon's competency to do a kidney transplant, we would expect that whether he/she had competence would be pretty much determined by that performance on the operating table; whether he/she had read at least two books on kidney transplants would be a meaningless measure, unless they demonstrated the ability to translate what had been read into surgical practice.)
2. It must focus on behavior that is capable of being observed. But,
3. It must not provide us with the lowest level of behavioral characteristics to assess, just because those are the ones that are more easily observable.
4. The competencies should relate clearly to the promotion of student learning.
5. The competencies should reflect the educational values to which we as professional educators aspire.
6. The instrument should emphasize the identification of strengths and weaknesses, as a springboard for growth, rather than merely record "passing or failing."
7. The instrument should be capable of use by the student teacher himself/herself for ongoing evaluation and growth (Wassermann & Eggert, 1976; 1994).

The work to develop such an instrument began with discussions with colleagues at the university, gathering data from their work in the preparation and assessment of student teachers. Following that was an examination of the literature in teacher education that dealt with the evaluation of student teachers. This also included an examination of the dozens of evaluative instruments that were available from other programs.

A list of competencies drawn from these sources emerged and seemed to distribute itself into three categories: teacher as role-model; teacher-pupil interactions (these were seen to create the conditions that would facilitate student learning); and the triangular relationship between teacher, students, and the curriculum. The problem of identifying each competency so that it would be observable without reducing it to the lowest level of performance was another challenge. For that reason, the idea of a "laundry list" type of instrument was rejected and instead a behavioral pattern model was chosen in which a particular teaching competency could be identified so that a profile of behavior would emerge.

To add to clarity of identification, it was decided to describe the behaviors in both negative and positive views. In the final culling, 19 items of teaching competency were selected, and behavioral profiles were developed for each, in positive and negative perspectives. In doing this, those "profile views" of teaching behavior seen as facilitating student learning while others were seen as dysfunctional was made explicit.

The next step was to field test the profiles. This was done with a sample of 100 student teachers. In this field test student teachers rated themselves on the instrument, along with ratings by their school associates (classroom teachers) and faculty associates (supervisors of student teaching). Additional data were collected through interviews with the student teachers, faculty associates, and school associates to obtain their feedback. Anonymous feedback from these three groups was also gathered. From these data, it was possible to discern which items produced a high level of discrepancy among the raters and all of these data were used in one more editing of the profiles.

When the profiles had been further refined, they were then subjected to an additional field test in which a reliability coefficient of +.70 was found among 20 raters who rated one student teacher.

The singular goal of the development of the profiles of teaching competency was to provide the student teacher and the program designers with a set of behavioral guidelines believed to be related to positive pupil learning outcomes. What's more, it was hoped that the profiles would provide the means by which student teachers would be able, from their first day in the classroom, to assess their own teaching behavior. As Wassermann & Eggert (1976) noted, "the most effective use of the Profiles will occur when (a) the student teacher rates him/herself; (b) supervisory personnel rate the student teacher; (c) all raters engage in a dialogue on each profile in an attempt to promote the student teacher's analysis of his/her performance, with a view toward improvement."

PROFILES OF TEACHING COMPETENCY

The results of the Wassermann & Eggert research yielded the Profiles of Teaching Competency, an evaluative instrument that continues to be used in the evaluation and growth of student teachers in the Professional Development Program at Simon Fraser University. Its emphasis is more on working toward growth and improvement than on the single criterion of pass or fail. The assumption made was that once strengths and weaknesses were identified, this would give the student teacher, the faculty associate, and the school associate the information needed that would lead to student teaching improvements.

The 19 competencies include:

I. The Teacher

The behavior is thoughtful
The behavior is self-initiating
He/she has a clear idea of his or her beliefs and those beliefs guide his/her actions.
The student teacher is a problem solver
He/she can put new ideas into practice
You can rely on him/her
The student teacher has a positive outlook

II. The Teacher and the Kids (Interactions)

He/she prizes, cares about, and values each individual
He/she knows how to observe, diagnose, and deal with students with behavioral difficulties
He/she uses clarifying responses in his/her interactions
He/she uses materials and classroom interactions that promote pupils' thinking
There's a lot of interaction among students in his/her class
He/she is a real person to his/her students

III. The Teacher, the Kids, and the "Stuff"—The Curriculum

The student teacher knows what he/she is doing in the classroom and it makes sense
He/she is knowledgeable in his/her field
He/she uses evaluation to promote learning
His/her classroom is a vital, alive, and zestful place
His/her teaching materials are varied, imaginative, and relevant
The student teacher unifies the group

TWO CENTS WORTH OF ADVICE IN
DESIGNING AN ASSESSMENT TOOL

If a faculty or a group of faculty members are in the process of designing an evaluative instrument to assess teaching competence, it might be advisable to consider some questions to serve as guidelines for the creation of an assessment tool. For example, does the instrument reflect the educational values of the program? Are those the behaviors that are truly prized in a teacher? In what way are the behaviors related to pupil learning? Does the evaluative instrument provide for continued self-scrutiny and professional growth?

If those questions can be answered in a way that seems satisfactory to the designers of the evaluative instrument, they may provide the guidelines that give some measure of confidence in creating an assessment tool.

Only when the goals are clearly defined can a program be structured and shaped to allow for the development of those competencies.

INTRODUCTION TO A TEACHING LIFE

In one of the more innovative teacher education programs in Canada, the three-semester Professional Development Program at Simon Fraser University begins with the radical idea of placing students immediately into public school classrooms. This initial practicum is carried out in teams of two. The teams are sent to a participating school, to observe and to play minor roles in assisting individual students, aiding the teacher in preparing teaching materials, assuming playground and recess duties, and perhaps, even working with small groups providing instruction in skills and comprehension.

Half of the first semester is composed of this in-school experience; the second half consists of on-campus seminars, where meaning is made by extracting it from real-life experience.

This immersion into classroom life introduces, by observation and practical experience, the professional tasks of teachers. It is upon this foundation that the coursework that follows is built. In other words, theory follows practice. When, for example, coursework addresses individual learning needs, or classroom management, or questioning strategies, or curriculum development, students' firsthand experiences in seeing these teaching strategies in operation provide the groundwork on which to build their knowledge and understanding. Theoretical constructs are not empty slogans and remote concepts; they are linked to what has been observed, and consequently, meanings are built from those real-life experiences.

Working with a teammate in these rudimentary beginnings is complementary; novice student teachers do not feel so alone or at sea. They have a buddy with whom to share ideas, frustrations, concerns; a partner with whom to build knowledge and understanding. As five-year-old philosopher Eli reminded us: "It's eeezier with a buddy."

When students begin their final practicum of 16 weeks of student teaching, they now face their assignments with considerably more knowledge, understanding, and implementation skills.

Can a more structured teacher education program provide some initial practicum experiences for their new students? Can a course be added to the existing list in which students are initially placed, for half a semester, in appropriate public-school classes, with a partner? Can this be followed by the second half semester, a time for "reflection on practice?"

Such an addition does not seem, at first glance, to be far-fetched; the pay-offs, however, could be substantial.

BUT WHAT IF?

But what if such an introductory course could not be added to the list of courses already required? What other types of primary experiences can new entry students use as a basis for the more cerebral studies that follow?

In any introduction to education course, a requirement can be incorporated that students spend x number of hours in classroom observations. They would be required to find their own schools, make their own arrangements to visit, sometimes with a letter of authorization from the faculty member or the dean of the School of Education to ensure that they were bona fide. In these days of high security around many schools, such a letter of authorization might be essential.

Students would not be parachuted in without prior preparation but given guidelines for their observations. For example, they might be asked to observe how teachers deal with presenting behaviors, how they handle "classroom management," what instructional strategies are used in certain academic areas, how groups are arranged, how teachers organize their time, and so forth. In the best of circumstances, classroom teachers might even offer to spend time after class, in responding to students' questions about what they have seen.

It is a given that such observations never involve making judgments about what has been seen, lest the doors to school observations be permanently closed. No teacher wants to put his or her teaching under the eyes of the Gestapo.

NOTES

The development of expertise in any profession requires—no, demands—a thoughtful, skills-oriented approach that has the best chance of promoting the competence believed essential for success in the profession. Can well-entrenched teacher education programs, that have been doing the same old same old things for too long, find within their ethos the desire and the effort to make changes so that there is a closer link between what they intend, and the means they use to reach those goals?

This chapter has suggested some alternatives. The following chapters continue to provide guidelines, strategies, and practical ideas to give a "leg up" for those who are not only interested in change but have what Jaime Escalante called the "ganas"—the desire—to follow through.

Chapter 3

To Know, to Understand, and to Know How

A Theoretical Framework

Change doesn't occur in a telephone booth when a meek person sheds his clothes, dons a cape, and becomes superhuman. It more likely comes through the planting of many seeds, only a small number of which will bear fruit. If a complete overhaul of a teacher education program is out of reach, perhaps the best we can do is make slow and incremental changes in which new ideas are put into practice, assessing carefully what has been done, adjusting, and making improvements along the way.

In this chapter, an instructional framework is being proposed that may be the equivalent of planting seeds. In lieu of a total upending of the entire structure of a teacher education program, this framework offers teachers a chance to redesign their courses in a way that leads students from knowledge gathering to the application of that knowledge to classroom practice. The framework may be applied to any course—be it "Human Development: Learning and Diversity," "Social Studies—Curriculum and Pedagogy," or "Mathematics—Curriculum and Pedagogy."

KNOWING, UNDERSTANDING, KNOWING HOW

The words "to know" are much stressed in educational practice and much coursework is tilted toward that goal. We want education students to know the curriculum standards for a given grade; the right answers to test questions; the way the internet breeds disinformation; the dates of important world events. But *to know* does not necessarily mean *to understand*. A child may know the names of the letters of the alphabet, but not understand how sounds are blended to form words. A student may know the mechanics of dividing fractions, but not understand about reciprocals.

Students may know the mnemonic HOMES to remember the initial consonants of the names of the Great Lakes but have no idea of what a "great lake" is, or where the lakes are located, or what their social, economic, political, or geographical importance is. Students may know that Columbus sailed across the Atlantic Ocean in 1492 and the names of his ships but have no deeper understanding of the implications of that voyage for the larger issues surrounding the "discovery" of the continent to the west of Europe.

Students may know that the Emancipation Proclamation was signed in 1863 but have no idea of how that impacted the lives of Blacks in the aftermath of the Civil War.

For students to "cross the bridge" from merely knowing to understanding, something more must occur beyond the act of simply gathering information—something that enables them to raise their level of knowing to understanding. To do that, students must learn how to put the pieces of information collected into a larger framework of understanding. Only a very few, very sophisticated students are able to make those connections on their own—from knowing to understanding, connecting the dots, the bits of information, so that they are able to see the larger picture.

In fact, most students need to be taken "across the bridge" from knowing to understanding, by giving them specific tasks that enable them to connect the dots. If students are to understand, to get the big ideas, teaching must incorporate the process of building the connections from knowing to understanding. Without their being given practice in making those connections, without those bridges, much of the information gathered is lost. What remains leaves students with a miscellanea of unconnected dots, bereft of their meaning. There is good reason that students lose 85 percent of the information "learned" after a two-month summer holiday.

Knowing how takes a step beyond understanding to applying what is known and what is understood. That is, putting ideas into practice. When we are able to apply understanding to the solution of problems, we advance further to the level of knowing how. Teaching students to *know how* involves giving them experiences in applying knowledge to the solution of practical problems. It means, for example, enabling them to apply the principles of electrical circuitry using batteries and bulbs to make a bulb light.

The inert knowledge of the rudiments of electrical circuitry does not result miraculously in students knowing how (Bracey, 1998; Shapiro, 1994). In order for them to know how, teaching must provide the further steps so that students may cross yet another bridge to that further level of cognitive development.

Teaching to *know* increases students' knowledge base. Teaching to *understand* enables them to make meaning from the knowledge gathered. Teaching to *know how* enables students to apply knowledge and understanding to the solution of problems.

Teaching to *know how* in teacher education must have a clear means/ends connection—that is, giving students opportunities to apply what has been learned and understood to actual classroom practice. This *knowing how* must proceed from prior experiences, rather than as "projects" that have no relationship to what has gone before. To tackle "applications" in the absence of *knowing* and *understanding* may result in inappropriate, unfounded, vacuous outcomes.

To achieve the goals of these three stages of intellectual development, teaching must provide learning experiences in all three areas, connecting them into an integrated whole.

In an example of that "disconnect," Leland (2016) has written, "Of all the hours I was at graduate school, I don't think there was all together an hour devoted to classroom management. We were developing beautifully crafted lesson plans that no one could use. I was learning esoteric phrases about test design. I spent two semesters doing a research project. I just wish somebody told me how to get a cellphone out of a kid's hands."

For preservice education students to wait until the last semester of coursework—student teaching—to apply what is known is too late. To assign students "projects" with no relationship to what has been learned and understood provides little help with practical application. Course design that can combine knowing, understanding, and knowing how in advance of student teaching will enable students to apply, more effectively, what has been learned in those preparatory courses.

The more students engage in these stages of their professional development, the more skillful they become in applying what they know and understand to the real life of the classroom. Like learning to play the violin, these preparatory learning stages cannot be single experiences, but must be allowed to develop and improve over time, thus ensuring that the preservice student is better prepared to become a more effective practitioner.

RE-CONCEPTUALIZING COURSE DESIGN

What is being proposed is not radical and surely many professors of education have come to the realization that a "teaching for thinking" (Wassermann, 2009) paradigm can be embedded into preparatory coursework for preservice teachers. But for those who have just joined the academy and those who are searching for better ways to prepare students to become more effective classroom practitioners, a framework for course design is being offered that takes a learner from gathering information by making observations (knowing) to analyzing information (understanding) to applying what is known to problem solving (knowing how). An added stage, *reflection on action*, requires the student to play an active role in the assessment of their work.

Thus, in learning new material, students would first begin with the gathering of data. This could be done through the viewing of a film or a video, examining an article or reading a story about a classroom event, studying a "profile" of a student presenting learning difficulties, examining data in a graph or a table, making real-life classroom observations, examining the construction of a teacher-made test, observing the behavior of a student over a period of time, examining a teacher's questioning strategies in a classroom observation, examining the nature of a student's computation errors in a math exercise, and so on.

The examples of the many ways in which students can gather knowledge through observing are extensive and varied and many curriculum experiences in virtually every education course can be introduced by asking that students to make observations of the kinds of tasks suggested above.

The second stage in the framework asks that students process the acquired information by using the thinking operations of comparing, classifying, looking for assumptions, suggesting hypotheses, summarizing, and/or interpreting data (Raths et al., 1986). These operations call for different ways and different opportunities for students to deepen their understanding by subjecting the information gathered to different kinds of analyses. At this stage of the learning experience, students might compare two teachers' questioning strategies; two studies of child behavior; a particular charter school and a public school; two ways of teaching beginning reading; two ways of classroom management; the lecture approach and the laboratory approach to teaching science.

They can classify the various textbooks used to teach beginning reading; common core standards for a particular grade level; social studies topics at the fifth-grade level. They can look for assumptions in children's test scores; in the advocacy of French immersion; in children's presenting behaviors; in disciplinary approaches; in teaching strategies; in curriculum objectives; in top-down reform efforts to improve schools.

They can suggest hypotheses to explain children's presenting behaviors; low test scores; parental involvement; reading difficulties; school absenteeism; failure of top-down reforms to improve schools; why some children continue to fail; student inattention. These are only a few examples of how data coming from observations can be analyzed. This kind of analysis serves to "build understanding." Students are aided in this process through the teacher's use of higher-order questioning (Wassermann, 2021) in *post hoc* discussions.

In the third stage of this framework, students are given opportunities to apply what they know—to put what they know into practice—creating the link between what has been observed and analyzed to classroom applications. This stage involves thinking at higher cognitive levels—i.e., problem solving, applying principles to new situations, decision making, designing projects, creating (Raths et al., 1986). Even outside the student teaching classroom, there are still ways for students to apply knowledge gathered and analyzed within the parameters of an on-campus course.

For example, students can create a YouTube presentation demonstrating effective classroom management; develop questions for a teacher interview about a topic relating to classroom practices and follow up by conducting the interview; write an in-depth analysis of efforts to reform educational practice over the last 50 years; create a dramatic presentation about a child presenting learning problems; create a computer program to provide information about higher-order questioning strategies; design an experiment to discover what science teaching methods work best with young children; develop a field trial program to assist reluctant readers; create a scrapbook with illustrations to show the major differences in educational approaches from 1900 to 2000.

These are only a few suggestions for the many and varied ways in which preservice students can be called upon to show how they may apply knowledge gathered and analyzed to educational practice. In furthering their work at this stage, teachers' use of higher-order questions once again plays an important role in enabling students' knowing how. One caveat about this third stage is not to set it in operation before the first two stages have been worked through and ensuring that the "applications" are consonant with and reflect what has been observed and analyzed.

Finally, providing students with opportunities to engage in self-assessment gives them practice in what is probably one of the more important aspects of professional development: "reflection on action." This is aided and abetted by the teacher's use of higher-order questions such as: What were the key points of what they did? What would they like to have improved? What new insights were acquired? What additional information could be gathered to enrich growing understanding and application? And of course, what are the criteria by which the students' assessments of their work are being made?

Promoting student reflection on their own learning experiences and making self-assessments revisits what has been learned, puts a student's work under his or her own critical eye, and opens the door to further inquiry. Rather than having the teacher do this evaluation, it puts the onus on students to become critically appreciative of their own work, thus setting in motion the process of self-examination and self-awareness, a dimension that we all hope future teachers will use as they attempt, each day, to put ideas into operation. This fourth stage uses the thinking operations of criticizing and evaluating and puts students on the pathway to becoming "reflective practitioners" of their own teaching.

Of course, it cannot be anticipated that every classroom situation that students will face will be dealt with in such preservice coursework. But even so, the proposed framework described above, at the very least, enables students to increase their knowledge base, deepens their understanding as they learn how to use that information in solving problems, and calls on them to become more reflective as they put their ideas into practice (Schon, 1983). It is no small gain when student learning and thinking are the beneficiaries and the boundaries of student intelligence are advanced.

PUTTING THE FRAMEWORK INTO ACTION

For a course in classroom management, Professor Carla Hicks has acquired a collection of what she calls "mini-cases"—brief studies of classroom management situations that a teacher might face in the course of a teaching day. Some of these mini-cases are written; some are short YouTube videos of actual classroom situations. Some might even involve a classroom teacher coming to talk to the students and presenting what was a problematic situation that he or she had to face.

One example of a written mini-case that Professor Hicks used follows.

She was phoned early Wednesday morning to substitute for a teacher who had just been taken ill. Could she arrive at school by 8:00 and be ready for the sixth-grade class? The regular teacher might be away for as long as a month. For an "on call" teacher, this was a plum assignment. She grabbed her bag of teaching materials—stuff she had accumulated as "fill in" activities for temporary work with classes she had no history with or any knowledge of, and headed out the door to Richmond Middle School, deep in the heart of the inner city.

The principal greeted her, glanced quickly at her youthful appearance, and expressed some trepidation. This was a tough class. Would she be able to handle it? She told him that her experience was neither long nor deep, but she would do her best. She was, after all, only three months out of her teacher education program and had had only four substitute teaching jobs, none lasting more than a few days.

Entering the room with her "bag of teaching tricks" she found few students at their own seats. Some of them were visiting with each other. One was talking on her mobile phone. Several were throwing a balled-up piece of paper around. The noise level was in the higher decibels and her immediate perception was that the class was in disarray. Her confidence began to slip as she put her teaching materials on the desk in the front of the room.

In a voice as loud as she could raise, she proclaimed, "My name is Celia Leland. I'm to be your teacher for today." No one paid any attention. It was as if she wasn't there. What was her next move?

At the first stage, Professor Hicks's students will have read the mini-case and talked together about their observations. This is better done in small groups, either pairs or trios, guided by a series of questions that focus the observations on key issues. For example:

- Using the data in the case, what observations can you make of this substitute teacher?
- What observations can you make about the principal?
- What observations can you make about the school?
- What descriptors can be attached to each? Make a list of them.
- Revisit your notes and look for value judgments and assumptions you have made. Think again and see if the data in the case warrant those assumptions and value judgments.

When the students have had time to engage with the case and the discussion questions, Hicks promotes further examination by calling for their observations, raising higher-order questions and responses to further probe their thinking. Have their discussions focused on the data? What assumptions have been made? What have they believed to be true that was not validated by the data? What value judgments have been made that go beyond the data?

The students are now asked to revisit their observations and discuss any changes that might be made as a consequence of their further examinations.

FROM OBSERVATION TO ANALYSIS

Once the students have had opportunities to complete their observations and to reflect on what they have observed, Hicks then uses the same mini-case to shift the focus of the activity to understanding what has been observed. This process of "making meaning" involves the higher-order thinking operations of interpreting data, comparing, examining assumptions, and suggesting hypotheses, thus setting the stage in preparation for the next step: applying what has been observed and understood.

This second stage, too, is enabled by the teacher's use of reflective responses and higher-order questions. But first comes the call for understanding through the interpretation of the data.

Hicks once again asks the students to form small study groups, either pairs or trios, to put their observations under critical scrutiny. A written task she has prepared calls for the following.

Based on the data you have gathered:

- What do you consider to be some key problems this teacher faces with this class?
- What hypotheses might explain the students' behaviors?
- To what extent, do you suppose, the students' behaviors are typical? Or singular?
- What do you consider to be the limitations and strengths of this teacher's ability to teach this class?
- What assumptions have you made about Celia Leland? What data in the case bear out such assumptions?
- Given these data, what strategies/teaching tools might Celia draw on to help her with this class? What assumptions are you making here?
- Based upon the data in the case and on your analyses, what suggestions would you make to the teacher to help her get through the first day of substitute teaching with this class? What assumptions are you making?

When the students have had a chance to discuss the analytical questions, the teacher then calls them together to debrief their analyses with the use of reflective responses and higher-order questions, thus setting in motion their preparation for the next stage: putting ideas into action.

FROM OBSERVATIONS AND ANALYSIS TO APPLICATIONS

In this third stage of this framework the teacher once again prepares a task for students to do in small groups, either pairs or trios. This task asks them to use the data they gathered in their observations and analyses to create some thoughtful and helpful suggestions for effective practice. For example:

a. Given the data, your observations, and your analyses of the situation, what would be the very first thing you would advise Celia to do in this classroom? To what extent is this suggestion consistent with the data and analysis?

b. Specifically, what steps should Celia be taking to bring about "order" to the room? What assumptions are being made?
c. Specifically, how should Celia interact with individual students? With the group?
d. What should a teacher do when faced with a group of students with whom she has no rapport, who she doesn't know, and with limited experience in teaching? What are your thoughts on this?
e. What might Celia have done in preparation for any substitute teaching assignment that might have prepared her more adequately for this class? What are your ideas about that?

This stage of instruction will, necessarily, take more time; students may also wish to refer to textbooks and other resources to help them formulate responses in their discussions, especially as they apply what is known to practice. When there has been sufficient time allotted for these group discussions, the teacher once again calls the class together to "debrief" the discussions and to generate thoughts, suggestions, and ideas about effective teaching strategies.

In these discussions, it would be important to ask students to "weigh" what they consider to be the effectiveness of the different proposals, and why they consider each to be more or less effective and how they might improve on them. This is done in the presence of reflective responses and higher-order questions, similar to those in earlier debriefing discussions. This debriefing also cultivates the process of students becoming more reflective practitioners, weighting and evaluating and assessing strategies and tools in relationship to the observed and analyzed data.

Not every classroom situation can be addressed in preparatory courses and every preservice student will, doubtless, face situations in their actual teaching practice that have not been examined in their coursework. But given their experiences in learning to gather and analyze data and in using these *a priori* strategies to make thoughtful and appropriate plans for classroom practice, such intelligent habits of mind will serve them well as they become more effective classroom teachers.

REFLECTION ON ACTION: CONDUCTING EFFECTIVE CLASSROOM DISCUSSIONS

Critical to the process of developing more effective classroom practitioners is the teacher's use of reflective responses and higher-order questions that put students' ideas and plans under critical scrutiny. Teachers who have studied how classroom discussions contribute to fostering students' intelligent habits of mind have identified what they consider to be the key conditions of productive discussions. These include the use of certain kinds of questions and responses that enable students to identify what they know, using that knowledge to understand the big ideas.

For "discussion teaching" to be effective, it demands the conditions that make it safe for students to become independent thinkers and problem solvers. Building a climate of trust, one in which students feel safe to offer their ideas, is the strong counterpart of the reflective responses and higher-order questions that make for more productive classroom discussions.

These essential conditions include:

- Listening to, attending to, and apprehending students' statements
- Giving students the time they need to formulate their ideas
- Being nonjudgmental in accepting students' responses
- Showing appreciation for students' ideas
- Focusing discussion on the examination of the issues rather than on finding the "right" answers
- Being comfortable with the lack of closure

a. Listening, attending, apprehending

On the surface, it seems a "no brainer" to ask that teachers listen and attend to what students are saying. However, given the pressures of classroom life it may be less than easy to pay full attention to listen, to attend, and to apprehend students' statements. Doing all of that requires teachers to focus attention fully on the student, shutting out other classroom noise. Eyes turned to the student, face showing interest, the teacher communicates with body language: "I am with you. I am listening to what you have to say. Your ideas are important to me."

Listening, attending, and apprehending means more than just hearing the words. It includes observing the behavioral cues as the words are being spoken, hearing nuance and voice inflection, observing particularly chosen words to express ideas, noticing where the statement is given emphasis. When all of that can occur, the teacher is doing what Freire (1983) calls "apprehending"—taking in and making meaning of the totality. Nothing gets in the way of full concentration on the student and what the student is saying.

When teachers can do this, it provides them with the information they need to formulate intelligent responses. It also creates a climate in which respect for students and for their ideas is palpable. And more, it contributes to the essential condition of interactive teaching—that is, the student and teacher are engaging in a dialogue in which all parties together are searching to understand, creating, in Christensen's (1995) words, a "community of learners."

b. Waiting for the students to formulate their thoughts

Teachers are more often than not in a race with the clock, trying to get all that needs to be "covered" completed by the end of class. However, if intelligent habits of mind are to be cultivated and fostered, teachers need to put aside the rush to finish and allow students time to think. This process cannot be bought cheaply. Thinking takes time. Good ideas take time to formulate. Unfortunately, we cannot have both speed and thoughtfulness.

c. Being nonjudgmental in accepting students' responses; appreciating students' ideas

Making it safe for students to express their ideas is at the heart of productive and intelligent classroom discussions. When students are fearful that their ideas are going to be penalized, few of them will risk offering them. If ideas are going to be rewarded, only those who are certain that they have the "correct answers" will volunteer them.

Judgments fall easily from teachers' lips, and some of us think that is a big part of the job (i.e., to tell students when they are right and when they are wrong). However, such judgments are anathema to a climate in which new and original ideas may flourish. This may be one of the more difficult principles of effective classroom discussions—that is, for teachers to say, "I see," rather than "That's good," or even "That's an interesting idea."

Avoiding judgments does not preclude showing appreciation for a student's contribution. Saying "Thanks, Megan, for contributing your ideas," is not only acceptable but a welcome input into the discussions. The caveat in showing appreciation is the teacher's genuineness in offering it. Anything that sounds phony or mechanical is counterproductive.

d. Discussions that focus on examining issues rather than on finding answers

One of the important conditions that make this "arm" of discussion teaching effective is the teacher's ability to operate in the realm of uncertainty. In this realm the emphasis is on examination rather than on finding the only acceptable answer. The ability to do this requires, at the least, a teacher's belief that this more open-ended discussion is of value.

The need for certainty—for the security that closure brings, seems to be a built-in feature of our human makeup. The human organism needs to resolve ambiguity. When closure is reached, it is accompanied by a palpable sigh of relief, a psychological "whew." Having answers gives security. Not knowing, for certain, having to weigh alternatives, to examine assumptions, to suspend judgment, provokes anxiety. It is undeniable. It feels good to know the answers.

It feels affirming when your students can tell you, with certainty, what it is you think they should have learned. It is much more stressful to have to take the risks in applying knowledge to figure out potential solutions to problems, where answers are rarely clear, where the meaning we make is our own, and where the best answer is often, "it depends."

Even experienced teachers who operate with a high tolerance for ambiguity often wish for the relief that a clear, definitive answer can bring. This is especially true for beginning teachers and preservice students who suffer from insecurities associated with their lack of experience and for whom "good answers" appear to reduce the stresses of teaching. Preservice students look to their teachers, to workshops, and to lessons to tell them, with certainty, what they think they need to know in order to teach well. But in the end, as most experienced teachers know, they are usually left to their own resources in figuring things out for themselves.

The bad news is that it is not the definitive answer that allows a student to progress from knowing to understanding and then to problem solving. Knowing definitive answers does not an educated person make, because knowing alone is far from a guarantee that a new teacher will behave intelligently, wisely, or competently.

Classroom discussions in which a teacher can approach a student's response and say, "Tell me more," or perhaps, "I'm wondering how you figured that out," or "Perhaps you have some data to support your idea," are all invitations for students to examine further. These questions/responses do not lead to answers; they call for further inquiry. They insist on clarity of thinking, upon reflection about a position, upon examples and data to support ideas. Such responses call for students' intelligent examination that leads to increased understanding and potential for considered action.

The absence of closure may, at first, be disconcerting for those new at such discussion strategies. Yet after time, many teachers find that relinquishing the need for certainty is wonderfully liberating.

More about effective teacher-student interactions is found in chapter 7.

NOTES

Long-term experiences with this framework—that is, proceeding from knowing, to understanding, to knowing how, to self-scrutiny, in the presence of higher-order responses and questions in discussions have provided an abundance of evidence to show that when this framework can used as a basis for teaching any preparatory course, it is a powerful strategy in its ability to transform students from "lesson learners" into thoughtful, considerate, more effective practitioners (Ewing, 1990). Teachers who have engaged preservice students in these ways have seen positive results not only in their classrooms, but also in work that carries over into teaching practice.

But make no mistake. Just as there is no free lunch, this approach has its caveats. There is a powerful force in play when teachers begin asking students questions, rather than setting themselves up as purveyors of truth. Students who experience the growing sense of personal power that such discussions bring are less likely to be blindly obedient, submissive, and complaisant.

On the other hand, if a teacher is insensitive and uses questions to interrogate, forgetting that a student has feelings, this can be damaging to the student's sense of self-worth, putting that student on the defensive, unwilling to take the risk of responding further.

And on the very last point it is important to remember that the key elements used in these classroom discussions are not necessarily in evidence every single moment of every class. There are times when teachers will want to tell their students what they think. There are times when teachers will make judgments. There are times when teachers will want students to know definitive answers. And there are times when teachers will disagree with students, give information, explain certain procedures.

In other words, there is a time for work that follows this proposed framework for course design that elevates students' intelligent habits of mind and leads them toward becoming more effective classroom practitioners. And there are times for other kinds of work. The art and skill of reinventing preparatory course design, and, in fact, the art of teaching, is for the teachers to know what their goals are and then to use those teaching strategies that are consistent with those goals, so that what teachers do is entirely congruent with what they hope to accomplish, consistently connecting their means with their ends.

Chapter 4

Some Radical Ideas

In chapter 3, a framework was proposed that would enable those responsible for teacher education courses to redesign what they do in order to connect their teaching goals more closely with their teaching strategies. Those suggestions are more easily implemented; outside of the classrooms of individual teachers, nothing is changed. The overall shape of the teacher education program proceeds in its "traditional" way.

Changing course design is not revolutionary. What is being suggested in this chapter is, in fact, revolutionary.

BEGINNING WITH STUDENT TEACHING

When the faculty of education at the then brand-new Simon Fraser University opened its doors in 1965, thirty-two intrepid students enrolled in the very new Professional Development Program. These were the few brave souls who found their way to the top of Burnaby Mountain, where the university was still under construction. The campus looked like an erector set with construction crews trying to put pieces together into familiar shapes. Finished classrooms were few and far between. Some of the rooms that had four walls lacked doors. The glass roof of the Academic Quad was yet to be installed and rain poured through, drenching anyone trying to get to class.

The newly appointed dean of education, Dr. Archie MacKinnon, came with a PhD from Harvard. His outline for the three-semester Professional Development Program was simple:

Semester 1: 8 weeks of student teaching followed by 8 weeks of on-campus seminars
Semester 2: 16 weeks of courses including lectures and seminars
Semester 3: 16 weeks of student teaching

It was left to the four newly hired professors of education to "put meat on the bones" of this very loose framework. All of them had come from traditional teacher education programs at colleges and universities in Canada and the United States.

When questioned by his newly appointed professoriate about the rationale for such a radical approach that began with a student teaching practicum, MacKinnon had a ready response. He claimed that many students came into teacher education without a real-life picture of what teaching was all about. Spending a year or two doing coursework, culminating with a student teaching practicum might be time wasted, if that student found, at the end, that he or she was not really made for a teacher's life. Beginning with student teaching would give students an immersion view—so that a life choice could be made sooner, rather than later.

It was a bold and, many thought, reckless notion.

Long-tenured professors at the sister institution across the city, the University of British Columbia, were loud and clear in voicing their objections: "We'll give that preposterous program six months—no more, before it is shown to be the colossal failure it is."

Principals and superintendents of schools across the province also voiced loud objections. "We are not going to place novice student teachers in classrooms in our schools. They are not adequately prepared."

Dr. John F. Ellis, the new chair of the education faculty, recognized the cries of alarm that were heard across the province. In response, he wisely hired a public relations officer from the Canadian Air Force, Jack Paterson, to visit school districts across the province, to see if they might be convinced to accept new student teachers.

Paterson, whose consummate human relations skills were unsurpassed, got in his car and proceeded to visit one school district after another in a province as large as the combined states of California, Oregon, and Washington. In his briefcase, he had two bottles of whiskey.

Coming into a superintendent's office, Paterson was greeted with, "No way. No way we're going to take your student teachers." At which point Paterson took out his bottles of whiskey, placed them on the superintendent's desk, and said, "Can we talk about it?"

This anecdote has been told many times, but it is worth repeating here because it gives hard evidence that radical changes in many fields, including traditional ones that have long endured and have become deeply entrenched, are often met with rejection, insults, condemnations, and predictions of hopeless failure. And it may take more than two bottles of whiskey to persuade those in positions of power to change and, at the very least, be persuaded to have another look at what's possible.

A RATIONALE BEHIND BEGINNING WITH STUDENT TEACHING

Despite all the naysayers, this radical notion became one of the more successful ideas of how professional training may proceed. More than MacKinnon's claim that neophyte student teachers would learn, in their first classroom trials, whether they truly wanted to become teachers, the initial practicum served as an important foundation for what was later studied in seminars. In other words, having initial practicum experiences laid the groundwork for students to better grasp important theoretical concepts that were dealt with in coursework.

Of course, initial practicum students did not, and were not required to carry out the higher-level professional tasks that more advanced student teachers were expected to do. But they were able to take on tutoring of individual students wrestling with learning difficulties, assist in preparing learning materials, provide a helping hand in supervising out-of-class trips, and other less demanding tasks. Moreover, they were able to observe how effective teachers carried out the many professional tasks that made up a teaching day.

It was the Nobel Laureate physicist, Richard Feynman (1984) who first described the advantages of such firsthand experiences on which larger theories and concepts could be built. As Feynman described it in his book, *Surely You're Joking, Mr. Feynman!*, "play" was the pivotal experience in enabling his thinking to move forward on the physics problem that eventually led to his receiving the Nobel Prize. In his provocative and delightful book, he wrote that where his work in physics followed a more rigid, structural pattern, he quickly became disenchanted with it, no longer taking any pleasure from the work. So he taught himself to play with physics, doing whatever he felt like doing, because "it was interesting and amusing for me to play with it."

In the cafeteria of Cornell University, much to the chagrin of his colleagues, he played with the dinner plates, actually tossing them in the air and observing their "wobble rate." As Feynman described it, "It was effortless. It was easy to play with these things. It was like uncorking a bottle. Everything flowed out effortlessly. There was no importance to what I was doing, but ultimately there was. The diagrams and the whole business that I got the Nobel Prize for came from that piddling around with the wobbling plates" (Feynman, 1985).

It may seem a reach to connect the "play" experiences of Feynman to an initial practicum for neophyte student teachers. Yet borne out with time, the initial practicum served not only the purpose of allowing students to "discover" whether teaching was actually for them, but it provided a grounding in the real life of the classroom, so that subsequent work on the larger concepts of "child development," "curriculum development," "instructional methods," "individual differences," "special needs," and other significant educational issues addressed in courses had greater meaning and the potential for greater understanding.

Moreover, these introductory experiences allowed for initial observations of what many in the profession consider some essential attributes of teacher-student relationships. Even though beginning student teachers could only carry out rudimentary tasks, supervisory personnel could quickly observe behaviors that were considered counterproductive to effective classroom practices.

So introductory student teaching experiences had considerable benefits—again, borne out over time. There is no longer need for a public relations person to approach school districts, hat in hand, pressing for placements for Simon Fraser student teachers. In fact, the opposite is now true.

A THIN ENTERING WEDGE

What would it take for a traditional teacher education program in an established university or college to begin with a student teaching experience? Are the 55-plus years of data from the highly regarded Simon Fraser University Professional Development Program sufficiently compelling to persuade professors of education to open a door to introductory student teaching?

In a teacher education program that consists of a series of required courses leading to the final practicum, it is not far-fetched to consider the inclusion of an introductory course, "Initial Student Teaching" or "Introduction to Student Teaching." Adding such a course is surely within the realm of the possible, provided the rationale for such inclusion is made clear.

At Simon Fraser, pairs of students are teamed to work in their initial practicum. Again, the rationale for this is clear. Students working as partners can share ideas, concerns, observations. They support each other through the trials and tribulations of newly experienced classroom life.

Working in pairs takes the stress off the individual and makes the experience less intimidating, less fearful, and more collaborative. Remember Eli's advice: "It's eeezier with a buddy."

STUDENT TEACHING SUPERVISION

Very few professors of education are willing, let alone eager, to take on the job of student teaching supervision. In most colleges and universities, this responsibility falls to teaching assistants—doctoral candidates who are given a small stipend for their work and perhaps tuition-free credits. Rarely is there any training or preparation for this role; the TAs are merely given a list of students and schools and left to their own devices. The results of such neglect are student teachers who slip through their practicum experience without much help or guidance from those who should be their primary sources of professional development.

In some of the more successful teacher education programs, experienced public school teachers are seconded from their classrooms for a *pro tem* appointment to the faculty, with the primary purpose of student teaching supervision. At Simon Fraser University, these professionals are called faculty associates. They are selected from a large group of applicants and are paid at the same rate as they would earn in their classroom teaching roles.

Before undertaking supervision, faculty associates attend workshops to develop competence in supervisory practice. These include providing them with a clearly articulated list of teaching competencies to focus on, plus some interpersonal skills training in evaluating what is observed.

With that grounding in specifics (i.e., what to observe and how to provide evaluative feedback, when each goes into a school), he and she knows what to look for and what better methods to use to provide that help. This, after all, is their primary role.

Faculty associates do more than supervise student teachers. They breathe fresh life into the professoriate, invigorating teaching practices and providing current and contemporary views of classroom life. For professors, many of whom have long been removed from public school classrooms, if they ever even were there, these classroom practitioners are a vital source of energy and commitment to teaching excellence.

Can a school of education find, within its budget, the resources to hire, on a temporary basis, school practitioners to supervise student teachers? At the bottom line, it comes down to what that faculty considers important in promoting the professional development of excellent teachers.

GRADING AND MARKING— A DIFFERENT PERSPECTIVE

This chapter has advocated some innovative ideas for the supervision of student teachers. And if the reader has not been sufficiently put off by this time, another even more radical idea is being presented in this last section of the chapter. It suggests that as an alternative to using grades for student teaching, students should be evaluated, instead, with pass-withdraw.

It is more than a half century since the faculty of education at Simon Fraser University introduced a proposal, first to the education faculty and then to the university senate, to change the grading system for student teaching to pass-withdraw. The chair at that time remembers it well. First there was the hue and cry among certain members of the education faculty who claimed that such a change would lower standards and ensure mediocrity. Having just passed with a tiny majority, the proposal went to the university senate, where once again the same objections were raised.

In the end, the senate reluctantly agreed to accept the proposal. And thus, beginning in 1968, student teachers were rated on a pass-withdraw scale. The "grade" of pass had to indicate that by the standards of teaching competence that were integral to the teacher education program, the student had, in fact, measured up, without qualification. A grade of withdraw indicated that a student would more likely be better suited in another profession. It should be noted that in lieu of fail, "withdraw" was used. In other words, it was not that the student was a failure; it was that teaching did not appear to be his or her best option for a future professional career.

Despite the hue and cry of those who believed that absent of grades the teacher education program would result in graduating mediocre students, the opposite, if anything, came true. In other words, the sky didn't fall. Pass-withdraw, in fact, ensured that student teachers completing the program continued to work toward developing those competencies that signaled their effectiveness as professionals. The primary objective was to become professionally competent, according to the program's criteria—not to get an A.

For a school of education to institute such a radical change is clearly not for the fainthearted. Surely other colleges and universities have moved in this direction without harming their reputations as first-class institutions of higher learning. There are important benefits for taking such a bold step. First, with pass-withdraw, the implicit emphasis is on the development of professional competence, not the acquisition of a high grade. Second, it removes from consideration the aggressive competition for a higher grade. Third, since grading is, if one is truly honest, specious and may have little or no relationship to professional competence, what's the real issue here?

NOTES

This chapter has presented several more revolutionary suggestions for changing, for the better, what is offered in teacher education programs, beginning with the radical notion of introductory student teaching. It also suggests the use of trained classroom practitioners for the supervision of student teaching as well as a change in the grading system for the practicum.

These ideas are further developed in chapter 9, which offers additional suggestions about how student teachers are assured the best and most effective practicums.

PART II
DEVELOPING COMPETENCE

Chapter 5

Introduction to Part II

To enumerate the many and various professional skills that teachers are required to use during the course of even one teaching day would involve a tome equal to the *OED*. That is why the following chapters have been selective in identifying those particular competencies that this writer considers to be essential in effective teaching—no matter what the grade level, the school, the student group. Doubtless this will cause hue and cry from the academy in pointing to what has been omitted and who have their own preferences about what should have been included.

Yet few will argue that teachers' ability to deal with presenting behaviors of students that address their learning needs, their ability to use classroom interactions that enable learning and promote critical thinking skills, and their skill in developing curriculum experiences that engage, stimulate, and extend knowledge and foster understanding of the big ideas are some of the key competences required of teachers. In addition, teachers must also confront the many and confounding challenges of today's classrooms; the demands on teachers are more extensive, more arduous, more exhausting than ever before.

That is why the next four chapters have been devoted to these competencies—not only describing them, but also suggesting instructional strategies in professional preparation that have a better chance of developing such competence.

DEVELOPING COMPETENCE: FROM KNOWING, TO UNDERSTANDING, TO KNOWING HOW

Each chapter begins with some of the more important ideas in the subject area—in other words, "what's important to know." This is followed by some suggestions for how instructors may promote the development of competence in these fields of knowledge. This can be done within the framework of existing course structures.

What is being presented in these chapters are some ideas, suggestions, and protocols for helping students to progress from knowing, to understanding, to knowing how. The suggestions are malleable and not writ in stone. They can be adjusted to meet the needs and the contents of specific courses, given the instructor's views of what can obtain, what needs to be modified, what needs to be omitted, what needs to be added. Paradigms are just that: suggestions for what is possible. It is left to individual instructors to make the best of what is here on offer.

Chapter 6

Developing Competence
Kids—Learning to Observe, Diagnose, and Deal with Individual Behavior

She had been identified in the school records as one of the students in most need of remedial help. Although now in seventh grade, her academic skills put her performance at about a second-grade level in reading, math, and other language arts areas. She had moved many times, and Meadowbrook Middle School was her 10th school in seven years. Moving around so much meant missing a lot of schoolwork—causing major gaps in her educational development.

She was often the butt of hurtful remarks from other students, her self-respect eroded from the punishing "blows" to her self-esteem suffered at the hands of peers and teachers each time she failed to know the answers, which was always. At the very bottom of the classroom power hierarchy, shame was her constant companion.

* * * *

He was new to the class, he and his brother having just arrived from El Salvador. The question about his immigration status was "iffy" but the school officials accepted his registration and placed him in Ellen Meyer's fourth-grade class. He spoke very little English—this small, underfed boy, with holes in his jeans and shoes, his dark eyes holding a thousand secrets. The principal had told Ellen that he was brought to the school by his brother; the parents were not on the scene. "I don't know what happened to him, but he hasn't been in the country very long. He's going to be a handful for you, I know."

Rudy took a seat near the windows, but quickly one of the boys near him said, "I don't want him sitting next to me. He stinks."

* * * *

When the principal asked her to come to see her after class, Julie Upton already surmised that the news would not be good. On Carol's desk was a large file folder that looked ominous. "I thought you should have a look at his file before you make up your mind to accept him. Cole is not just a disturbed eight-year-old. He's probably the most difficult challenge you will face as a teacher. I'm afraid if we don't do something for him, he's going to wind up as a statistic."

Julie picked up the folder. Clipped to the inside cover was a copy of a newspaper article, headline screaming: SEVEN-YEAR-OLD ATTEMPTS SUICIDE.

The boy's history was something out of a horror movie. He had been abused physically and sexually by his biological father, who was now in prison for raping two teenage girls. A physically small, red-headed boy who "looked like an angel," Cole might well be the single greatest challenge for this third-grade teacher.

WHAT'S IMPORTANT?

The spectrum of observable and subtle behaviors of students in today's classrooms have never presented more challenges than for today's teachers. Besides having to "teach the curriculum" and bring students up to state and provincial standards, the complexities of what some children reveal in terms of their observable behaviors are problems that would confound a Solomon. It would be a mistake to think that such problems exist only in inner city schools, where, of course, they appear in abundance. They are also seen in schools in the more "upper class" neighborhoods, although perhaps in different garbs.

A course that is usually required for all preservice students in a teacher education program is one that addresses child growth and development. Its essential features would normally include the developmental stages of growth, from early childhood to the teen years. In some courses, students would be required to "know" about significant growth features, including when children normally begin walking, talking, putting sentences together; when they become more independent; when they begin to develop maturity; the onset of puberty; the challenges of the teen years.

Knowing all of that doesn't help much in dealing with the kinds of behaviors in evidence in many classes. For example, children whose parents are single and struggling; who are hungry; who live in fear of being deported; whose father/mother is on drugs; who are excessively dependent, passive; who are "out of it"; who are filled with anger; who reveal racist tendencies; who have borne the brunt of racism; who are physically handicapped and need special care and attention; who don't speak English; who are convinced that vaccines are harmful; and more.

Add to all of that is the long hiatus of missed school days, due to the stay-at-home year of COVID-19. It would not be an exaggeration to claim that any of these singly or in combination would play havoc with a child's ability to learn.

What, then, would be some important ingredients in a course in child growth and development that would enable preservice students to know, to understand, and to know how to deal with, at the least, some of these issues? These could include the following types of learning activities:

a. To know: The students might begin with learning to make careful and value-free observations about the presenting behaviors of a pupil, with the proviso that observations are based on what is seen and not on specious judgments.
b. Promoting understanding: A next step would be for students to gather additional data about the pupil that would lead to some insight with respect to the roots of, and the conditions contributing to these behaviors. These data would lead to the generation of a working hypothesis that would not only point to what lies "behind" the presenting behaviors but also suggest effective teaching strategies.
c. Knowing how: The students would now use the data gathered to develop a teaching plan—a plan that would be consonant with what has been learned and understood about the pupil, and that addresses the pupil's singular learning needs. At this point, students would also be asked to consider what, if any, of their own beliefs, attitudes, and values might get in the way of their successful implementation of the teaching plan. As well, the student might consider what, if any, conditions or circumstances might delimit the carrying out of the teaching plan.

Finally, it would be essential for students to understand the limitations under which they are operating. Doing the best one can, following the guidelines above, does not necessarily lead to "fixing" what is wrong in a child's life. Teachers do the best they can, with the constraints under which they work. To expect perfection, to expect a happy ending, is for Hollywood and not for teaching practice. A teacher who expects happy endings may be in the wrong profession.

Sometimes, in the best-case scenario, a teacher may "give" a distressed pupil a good year—a year of safety, of protection, of care, and of opening some avenues of thought. And as little as that might sound, it is, nevertheless, a goal worth prizing.

KID'S KITS: EFFECTIVE STRATEGIES FOR PROMOTING COMPETENCE

One way to promote students' learning to know, to understand, and to know how to deal effectively with children's behaviors that impede learning is being in a real classroom—to be a "fly on the wall" whose single mission is to see, to discern, to apprehend not only the presenting behavior but also the more subtle signs of what is going on. Failing that, the use of simulations, of "kid's kits" can be a viable alternative.

Using "kid's kits" allows for the incorporation of the three essential elements in the instructional framework: knowing, understanding, and knowing how. One way this can be done is for the instructor to design "mini-cases" of pupils, with descriptions of presenting behavior, as well as including supporting data. In this learning process, the student reads the behavioral description, uses that to generate a working hypothesis about what the behavior communicates, and identifies the kind of information needed to support or contravene the hypothesis.

Supporting data containing the information sought are also included in the "kid's kit." As the student continues to develop a more informed hypothesis, he or she examines the supporting data and thus works to refine the hypothesis. In that process, the working hypothesis becomes more informed, and thus more helpful in pointing to potential teaching strategies.

The last stage of this process is for the student to use all of the data, including the working hypothesis, to come up with an instructional plan that addresses the particular and singular learning needs of the student. One important adjunct to this process is for the student to become more intimately aware of his or her own biases, predispositions, and beliefs that might get in the way of implementing that learning plan. It is also of benefit when two or three students work on one "kid's kit"—sharing information, ideas, suggestions and keeping each other on track.

Not to be neglected is the instructor's suggestions for background readings that may inform the students' knowledge and understanding at any stage of his or her work on the kid's kit.

A course instructor has several options in assessing students' understandings and knowledge about human growth and development and the behaviors that affect learning. One, of course, is the sharing of these materials in small and large group discussions, where questions are put to the students about not only the process of gathering information but also how that information led to a teaching plan. Another is for the course instructor to read students' responses and assess them according to course criteria. There are doubtless other ways; the important criterion is, of course, providing the feedback that further informs students' learning.

KID'S KIT: EXAMPLE

Classroom Observation of Brian—a Seventh-Grade Student

Brian's behavior is extremely aggressive. He is constantly off task and when reprimanded, he shouts out responses that are rude and often profane. Without provocation, Brian can leap out of his seat, acting out behavior that he might have seen in a movie: random movements of arms, legs, and head, incoherent speech—as if he is playing a role. During class discussions his outbursts are loud, ill-mannered, and vulgar. When at his seat, he spends time looking out of the window or drawing sexually explicit figures in his notebook. His work is never completed and he seems indifferent to the teacher's insistence that he needs to work harder if he is going to pass. He is a loner; the other children avoid him.

Student's Observations of Brian's Behavior

Brian is a seventh-grade boy whose behavior in class is extremely aggressive. He acts out, calls out with profanity, and doesn't seem able to do his schoolwork. He seems indifferent to the teacher's reprimands and has few or no friends in class.

Background Data

Brian Wilson is a seventh-grade student at the Woodward Middle School in the tree-lined, suburban school district of Upper Plains. Brian's parents had recently been divorced and he is now living with his mother and her live-in partner. Brian's father, a successful attorney, had left Brian's mother to live with a young woman whom Brian calls "my father's bimbo." He refers to his mother's new partner as "that a--hole." Brian's school records reveal that neither of his parents had wanted custody of him when their marriage broke up, but that Mrs. Wilson finally agreed that Brian could live with her.

Dr. Jennings, the school counselor, wrote that Brian's intelligence "fell into the normal range" but that his achievement was erratic. He also added that Brian's outbursts were "attention-seeking behaviors" and that he was troubled because he believes that neither of his parents want him.

Student's Working Hypothesis

Student's response here

Supporting information: What books, journal articles, consultations have helped you to understand more about Brian's presenting behaviors, create a viable working hypothesis, and create an instructional plan?

Student's response here

Instructional Plan and Expectations

Student's response here

Personal Beliefs/Feelings that Might Impede My Work with Brian

Student's response here

NOTES

"What do you do about a child who . . .?" is one of the most frequently heard questions from student teachers anxiously seeking more effective methods of working with individual students. Children's classroom behavior is often puzzling, exasperating, and exhausting, and acting-out behavior may drive student teachers to the very limit of their patience. Yet behavior is the way that most children send messages to others about how they feel and what is going on inside their heads and hearts.

When student teachers can learn to "read and interpret" behaviors more knowledgeably and with greater insight, they might have a better chance of understanding what the child is "telling" us behaviorally, and consequently choose better and more effective ways of helping that child to learn. Although not all children's problems are "fixable"—that is, within the sphere and influence of teachers and schools—there are many more children who might be helped if student teachers could learn to free themselves from facile judgments and apply greater wisdom in reading and interpreting children's behavior.

Using simulations like "kid's kits" should challenge student teachers' thinking about behavior, promote understanding about gathering relevant data to generate working hypotheses, free them from making gratuitous and simple-minded assumptions, and in general, provide for deeper awareness of classroom behavior and effective teaching plans. They provide the opportunity for student teachers to work from observing, to understanding, to applying what is known in actual practice.

Chapter 7

Developing Competence
Teacher-Student Interactions

The seventh-grade students were engaging in a discussion about the COVID-19 pandemic and how it was related to the Spanish flu that was responsible for the deaths of more than a half-million people in the United States. Sally Gardner, their teacher, wanted to highlight the importance of taking precautions that would help to prevent the spread of the disease, precautions that were overlooked in the case of the Spanish flu.

Because COVID-19 was an urgent and "close to home" concern, the discussion was heated and many students wanted to voice their ideas. There was no dearth of hands vying for "airtime."

"Okay," Gardner said. "I've heard from many of you about the steps we might take in order to keep us safe. And many of the ideas you have offered seem to me to be responsible and reasonable and in keeping with the recommendations of the doctors and scientists who are tracking the disease. Does anyone else have something to add?"

Malcolm, who had been quiet during the discussion, didn't raise his hand, but blurted out, "I think the whole thing is just a big lie. The vaccinations are just a way of making more money for the government and of scaring people. My folks are not getting the vaccine, and neither am I. And wearing a mask is just plain stupid. I know this is true because I read it on the internet."

* * * *

Which one of a dozen different responses should Sally Gardner make to Malcolm? How will her response enable Malcolm to think more about what he has suggested without demeaning him? How will her response affect his attitude toward school and his teacher? How will her response encourage his further understanding of the difference between truth and disinformation? Will she reflect what Malcolm has said, accepting his statement? Will she raise a question that asks him to think beyond his surface statement? How will she manage her own feelings in the face of his reliance on disinformation? These questions lie at the heart of the interactions that teachers use in classroom discussions.

Teachers interact with students hundreds of times each day, choosing from an extensive repertoire of options, from those that respond to an individual student's learning needs, to a student's behavior, to organizational and management concerns, to a student's logic in his/her thinking. For whichever response a teacher makes, it will inevitably have a different effect on students' thinking, their sense of personal power, their attitudes about school, teachers, and subject, and their feelings of safety in responding to a teacher's questions.

At their most effective, teachers' responses are singularly appropriate to their appreciation of a student's learning needs at that particular moment.

So what response should Sally Gardner make to Malcom? As in most other decisions that teachers make, "it depends." It depends on whether Ms. Gardner wishes to address Malcolm's belief in the truth of the internet, his willingness to take a stand against the rest of the class, his lack of trust in the best medical advice, and equally important, how she will be able to manage her own feelings about Malcolm's dogmatic insistence on bad information.

At the very least, Sally Gardner's response should be respectful of his feelings and of his statement; it should never demean. Whichever response Gardner chooses should, at the very least, attempt to open his mind. The response should also attend to what Malcolm has said; he must know that she has heard him. When these conditions can be met, she has several options that can be helpful, both psychologically and academically additive.

A teacher's response can be for better or for worse, helpful or hurtful. Using responses that enable and empower, that build students' self-esteem, that ask them to think logically and rationally is a sophisticated teaching skill. It is one of the consummate skills of effective teachers, and one that is largely neglected in teacher preparation programs.

What follows in this chapter are some suggestions for the ways in which, within a course structure, preservice students may begin to understand the nature and importance of teacher-student interactions, how questions and reflective responses are used to promote thinking, and how they might learn to use them effectively in teacher-student discussions. In other words, what follows adheres to the instructional framework of taking students from knowing, to understanding, and to knowing how.

But first: How might Sally Gardner respond to Malcolm?

You've gotten some information about the virus from the internet, Malcolm, and your ideas seem very different from the others heard in this discussion. I wonder how you could explain that? (Respects Malcolm's statement; uses a reflective response to show she has heard him and uses a higher-order question to raise his level of awareness.)

Or, *You've heard from the internet that the virus is a hoax. Many of your classmates disagree with you. I wonder how we could figure out who has the correct information?* (Respects Malcolm's statement; highlights the discrepancy between his statement and the others from his classmates; raises a higher-order question asking him to think more about what has been asked.)

Or, *Your information suggests that the virus is a government plot. Can you tell me how you came to believe that?* (Reflects Malcolm's statement and raises a higher-order question to ask him to think further about his ideas.)

Each of these responses is respectful of Malcolm's ideas and does not dismiss them. Each asks him to probe more deeply and to offer supporting data to confirm his ideas. None of them demeans him. Sally Gardner has refrained from making a judgment or revealing her own feelings about Malcolm's statement.

On the other hand, responses that would be diminishing, disrespectful, and not helpful might include the following:

Come on, Malcolm. No one believes what you read on the internet.

That's a pretty silly idea, Malcolm. I wonder why you choose to believe what everyone knows is wrong?

Malcolm, if everyone believed that, we'd all be in a big pickle and everyone would get sicker and sicker. Do you want that to happen?

None of these responses have the potential of helping Malcolm to reevaluate his ideas and consider an alternate point of view. In fact, they may further reinforce his position and make him more defensive and more intractable in his thinking.

Using appropriate responses that ask students to think, to reconsider their ideas, to use data to back up beliefs and opinions, opens the door to developing students' intelligent habits of mind. How teachers interact with students not only has profound effects on students' learning. These interactions also contribute to the quality of life in the classroom.

TWO ESSENTIAL INGREDIENTS IN TEACHERS' RESPONSES THAT CALL FOR FURTHER INQUIRY

While, on the surface, the notion of "attending" to what a student is saying might seem simplistic, it is, oddly, a greatly overlooked tool in human interactions. It is the very first condition that lays the groundwork for effective teacher responses. Attending means listening very closely to what the pupil is saying. It means "clearing your mind" of extraneous "noise" so that you may apprehend the surface and underlying meaning of the statement.

It involves more than just listening. It means hearing not only words, but nuances of expression, picking up on the affect so that the statement is heard in context. It means freeing oneself from the desire to comment or to judge it. A teacher attending and apprehending what the pupil has said provides that teacher with the "working material" to form an effective response.

A second ingredient is the teacher's ability to use what the pupil has said in formulating a response. There are, of course, many possible responses, and the response chosen should reflect the teacher's objective. Whichever response is chosen, it should, at the very least, communicate respect; be absent of judgment in word or tone of voice; apprehend what the pupil has said; enable the pupil to feel safe, non-threatened and non-defensive. In a dialogue where the aim is to promote pupil thinking and build intelligent habits of mind, teachers use all of the above in conjunction with higher order responses/questions.

The kinds of responses presented below are varying degrees of "higher-order responses and questions"—some less challenging, and others highly challenging. All of them, used in the presence of the above conditions, ask students to inquire further into their ideas.

Responses That Ask a Student to Reexamine His or Her Idea (Least Challenging)

Paraphrasing
Interpreting
Asking for more information (e.g., "Tell me a little more about that," or "Help me to understand what you mean.")

Responses That Call for Analysis of an Idea (Moderately Challenging)

Can you give me an example?
What assumptions are you making?
What alternatives have you considered?
How does what you have said compare to what _____ has said?
How might that data be classified?
What data support your idea?

Responses That Are Highly Challenging

What hypotheses can you suggest to explain it?
How have you interpreted that data?
How can you verify the authenticity of that data?

What criteria are you using in making those judgments?
What predictions can you make based on the data you have gathered?
How would you go about testing that theory?
What new scheme or plan can you envision for that situation?

Responses That Diminish Student Thinking

Agreeing or disagreeing with the pupil
Leading the pupil to the teacher's point of view
Offering a personal opinion
Giving advice
Talking too much
Challenging the statement harshly, which puts the pupil on the defensive

There are also responses that are intimidating, such as heckling, being sarcastic, or demeaning the student's ideas. These should be avoided; they do little more than create a climate of fear among students, making an open and productive discussion impossible.

Teachers who are able to make effective use of interaction skills in their teaching create a classroom climate in which students learn to make intelligent meanings from data and become habituated to rely on their cognitive resources to solve problems and make decisions. It is, in virtually all school district goals statements, the one that is high on the list of important educational objectives.

As students engage in learning to use effective teacher-student interactions, they begin to appreciate the importance of listening to self in the teacher-student dialogue. That self-scrutiny involves being open and non-defensive in their attempt to bring consistency between what was intended and what was actually spoken.

No one said it was easy. But it is these more challenging tasks that offer the most benefits in providing the best kinds of learning opportunities for pupils at every grade level.

FROM KNOWING, TO UNDERSTANDING, TO KNOWING HOW

If we could have it all ways, it would be more effective for teacher education programs to include a full semester's course in the study and practice of teacher-student interactions. Failing that, studies of teacher-student interactions may be incorporated in courses in human growth and development, educational psychology, or courses that dwell on teaching strategies.

Effective training in student-teacher interaction strategies would necessarily incorporate elements of knowing, understanding, and knowing how.

1. Knowing and Understanding

a.

If at all possible, students should begin studying interactions by observing what a teacher does when that teacher uses attending skills to inform his or her responses. This can be done with a prepared video of a classroom discussion or a one-on-one dialogue. The video needs only a single preparation and once made, it can be used and reused in subsequent sessions.

After viewing the video, students are then asked to make observations about the nature of the discourse, how they viewed the teacher's attending and apprehending interactions, and what they saw as the result of those responses on the pupil's subsequent responses.

To heighten this awareness, two videos can be made and compared, one in which the teacher is responding effectively and the other in which the teacher lacks skill in attending. The students are then asked to make comparisons about what has been observed in both and how they see the effectiveness of each in promoting pupil learning.

When it is not possible to use a video stream, transcripts of teacher-student discussions are a possible alternative. As teaching tools, they are not as powerful as videos, but better than nothing.

b.

A next step in promoting knowing and understanding is for students to practice formulating responses in a "pencil and paper" task. An example of such a task might look like Worksheet 7.1 (see page 59).

2. Knowing How

a.

Knowing how begins with students practicing these skills in role-playing contexts, with a partner or in a trio with their classmates. Working with a partner is more intimate, but working in a trio allows for the inclusion of a "monitor" who would observe and provide feedback to the role-playing teacher. In a trio, each would take turns playing each of the roles: teacher, student, and monitor.

Worksheet 7.1, Practice in Responding

In this practice task you are asked to formulate responses that ask pupils to examine their ideas, enabling them to think about them and reflect on their meaning. Your response should attend to the pupil's statement, show respect for the idea, and provide the means for the pupil to reconsider, reexamine, or extend on his or her thoughts.

a. Pupil statement: Squids are dangerous. They have tentacles that can kill you.
Your response:

b. Pupil statement: I know that people who were most affected by the COVID virus were those who lived in congested areas where the disease could spread more easily.
Your response:

c. Pupil statement: It was the tradition in Ancient China to bind the feet of women. Their feet got shriveled up and they couldn't walk. It was very painful.
Your response:

d. Pupil statement: The Canadian government set up residential schools for the Indians and they were taken from their homes so that they would learn the white culture.
Your response:

e. Pupil statement: I just read that the Harry Potter books were banned from the library in Nashville because they use curses and spells. I think that's stupid.
Your response:

f. Pupil statement: I read that during the Crusades, the men went about killing and slaughtering Muslims because they were considered heathens who didn't believe in the true faith.
Your response:

g. Pupil statement: Women didn't get the vote in the United States until 1919? They must have thought women were too stupid to vote.
Your response:

Providing support for these role-playing dialogues is a "study sheet" to which students can refer to remind them of the key features of effective responding. Study Sheet 7.1, below, is one example of what can be used.

Each "role play" is followed by a "debriefing," in which the participants provide feedback to each other. Each student should be able to participate in the discussion, giving feedback regarding the effectiveness of the "teacher's" skills in carrying out the dialogue. Not to be neglected is advice to the "teacher" on what he or she might do to improve in the next simulation.

The more these "role-play" dialogues can be carried out in the presence of *post hoc* reflection on the practice session, the more students will gain experience and expertise in their interaction skills that meet the criteria for effective classroom discussions.

b.

The next step at the *knowing how* stage is for the trios to reconvene, but this time in the presence of video or audio recording. Given the omnipresence of mobile phones that can record voice and image, getting the hardware to do the job is as easy as looking into a student's pocket. The trios now resume practicing, listening to the discussion afterward, in which all participants provide feedback. The first person to respond should be the "teacher."

Study Sheet 7.1, Training in Attending

Your ability to attend thoughtfully and perceive accurately—to apprehend—increases when the following conditions are met:

You can make and hold eye contact with the student.

You can listen and communicate respect for the student's ideas.

You can free yourself from the need to evaluate the student's ideas, either in tone or word.

You are able to make meaning of—to apprehend—what the student is saying.

You have an awareness of affect (verbal or nonverbal) being communicated by the student.

You are aware of indicators of stress.

You can formulate responses that accurately and sensitively reflect the meaning of the student's statement.

You can make the "pupil" feel safe, non-defensive, and non-threatened throughout the dialogue.

Here again, a "study sheet" enables a more productive analysis of the "teacher's" responses. This follow-up analysis zeroes in on those attributes of the discussion that are essential components of more productive interactions. An example of such a self-examination study sheet is offered in Study Sheet 7.2 (see pages 62–63).

NOTES

The work in developing more skillful teacher-student interactions is rooted in the theory that human interactions have power. They have power to nourish, to add substantially to the way people feel about themselves, to their ability to use intelligent habits of mind to solve problems and make decisions, to promote their independence. They also have power to hurt, to diminish a person's feelings about self, to stifle his or her thinking, to foster dependency on others. Words can communicate caring, thoughtfulness, respect. They can also belittle, ridicule, and reject.

When education professors are committed to the development of their students' interactive skills, such work may begin by attention to the guiding principles articulated in this chapter. This can be followed by allocating time for practice sessions and encouraging students to commit to a lifetime of self-scrutiny of their interactive style. Like other essential teaching skills, this is developed more on the job than in the preservice classroom. But the preservice classroom sets the stage for the important work that follows.

If the art of developing effective student-teacher interactions may be compared to making music, then these practice tasks are at the level of learning the notes. Using them in concert is what elevates skill to art. That is why the ingredient of learning to listen to self in the act of responding to pupils is the key to ongoing professional development of their interactive skills.

It is, of course, for professors of education to decide, for themselves, whether these skills are important enough to devote perhaps not a course, but a part of a course to their promotion and development.

Study Sheet 7.2, Examining My Interactions

As you listen to (or watch) the recording of your interactions, check on the line below the response you hear yourself making to the "pupil." Then, when you have finished checking your responses, write a sentence or two that points you in the direction of your next steps in the improvement of your interactive skills.

Responses that bring closure:
   Agrees with the student.
   Does not give the student a chance to think.
   Tells the student what the teacher thinks.
   Cuts the student off.

Responses that are intimidating:
   Heckles; is sarcastic; puts down the student's idea.

Responses that limit student thinking:
   Looks for single correct answer.
   Leads the student to "right" answer.
   Tells the student what to do.
   Gives information.

Responses that encourage reexamination of the ideas:
   Paraphrases the student's idea.
   Interprets what the student has said.
   Asks the student to give more information (e.g., "Tell me more about what you mean").

Responses that call for analysis of the idea:
   Asks for an example.
   Asks for any assumptions that have been made.
   Asks about alternatives that have been considered.
   Asks that a comparison be made.
   Asks how the data can be classified.
   Asks what data support the idea.

Responses that challenge:
   Asks for hypotheses to explain what the student is offering.
   Asks that data be interpreted.
   Asks for criteria to support a judgment.

Asks how those principles can be applied in a new situation.
Asks how the theory might be tested.
Asks how the plan could be implemented.

Responses that accept the student's idea nonjudgmentally:
I see.
Thank you.

Summary: Based on the data above, what insights can I draw about my interactive responses and what do I need to concentrate on in my next practice session?

Chapter 8

Developing Competence
The Teacher as Curriculum Maker

There are many courses in teacher education programs that address curriculum—especially as curriculum is related to specific subject areas. So it would not be strange to find, included in the list of required and elective courses, those that focus on language arts, math, social studies, and science, to name a few. These courses are intended to give preservice teachers a view of what is expected as they face the scholastic and standards-based requirements for the various elementary grades. The preparation for secondary teachers is more likely to include a strong focus on courses in the particular subject area in which the student is preparing to teach.

Despite the hours of preparation in these courses, it is not unusual to find new and even experienced teachers clinging to the manual of instruction to guide them in delivering the required curriculum for the grade. Most of the time spent in these preparatory courses is on listening to professors advocate what should be done—building knowledge, and perhaps understanding, but absent of knowing how. If it is true that the critical content is the process through which learning occurs, it is no wonder that students graduate from teacher education programs teaching not as they are told how to teach but as they themselves have been taught.

"Teaching as telling," long in fashion at virtually every stage of education, depends on students who are content to be passive listeners, disengaged from any requirement that they actively process the material and learn to use it effectively in their own teaching. In these contemporary times when even three-year-olds have their own tablets, and older children make their own Tik-Tok and YouTube videos, design their own websites, and have more familiarity with IT than many teachers, such an approach to curriculum is less than worthless; it is deadening.

In this chapter the focus is on preparing preservice students to develop curriculum, in any subject area, at any grade level, that will engage students actively, develop their cognitive skills, teach them to work collaboratively with each other, and extend their understanding of the important concepts, the "big ideas" in the curriculum. In other words, the "medium is the message."

The chapter provides a template for how this is done by giving examples of "practice tasks" that demonstrate how students may apply their understanding to actual classroom practice.

ESSENTIAL ELEMENTS IN CURRICULUM DESIGN: KNOWING AND UNDERSTANDING

a. What's the Big Idea?

Developing curriculum plans for pupils, at any grade level, begins with the identification of the "big ideas"—that is, those essential concepts from which the rest of the curriculum plan evolves. Big ideas give shape to the curriculum experience. They point to what is important to know and to understand. They not only guide the development of the curriculum plan, but they also give shape to any teacher-student discussions.

So what are big ideas?

First, they make statements rather than ask questions. Even a cursory glance reveals their intrinsic energy; we know that they matter. Some have moral and ethical implications. Some focus on current issues; some with historical events; some with scientific concepts; some address the fine and performing arts.

From where do they come? They may come from classroom texts, from curriculum guides, from the standards and benchmarks of state and ministry departments of education. They may arise from concerns of students or teachers, from current events, history, the media, community affairs, politics, or the day-to-day experiences of students.

Some examples of a few big ideas are:

- Machines make work easier for people. In making work easier, they may displace workers from their jobs.
- Various fuel sources produce energy. In many cases, the energy they produce creates harmful effects on the environment.
- Understanding nutrition does not necessarily lead people to make better choices about what they eat.
- People write or tell stories to give us information, to entertain and amuse, to make us think, and to give us pleasure.

- The internet is a valuable source of gathering data. It also generates false information coming from anyone with a bone to pick and access to the IT world.
- Making evaluative judgments is influenced by the particular opinions and beliefs of the "judge." Evaluative judgments are not truths.
- In a democracy, people get to choose their leaders by the process of election. "Propaganda" is one way that influences how people vote.
- The coronavirus has had a major effect on the economy as well as on the health of a large portion of the population in many countries.

If an idea is too broad in scope, it may be too abstract or cover too much territory to lead to productive classroom study. They may be more "topics" than big ideas. For example:

- Natural resources are finite.
- Prejudice breeds hatred.
- All sea life is interdependent.
- Culture is learned.
- Animals and plants adapt and change to survive in different environments.

If an idea is too limited in scope, it may focus on small pieces of information and not lend itself to substantive inquiry. For example:

- Magnets have two poles, one called north and one called south.
- Ice is frozen water.
- Frogs hatch out of eggs.
- Online learning helped students to keep on top of their studies when schools were closed.
- Shells are the outside vertebrae of marine animals.
- The heart pumps blood throughout the circulatory system.

Choosing the "big idea" that is the starting point in the development of a curriculum plan requires the teacher's first consideration of what he or she wants the students to know, to understand, and to know how in this particular curriculum area. When teachers are clear about this, this clarity guides their formulation of the big idea. Once the idea is identified and articulated, the curriculum plan can begin to take shape. Teaching to examine big ideas is at the heart of any curriculum plan.

*b. Knowing and Understanding: Shaping the Curriculum
Plan with an Emphasis on Higher-Order Thinking*

For many preservice and new teachers, designing curriculum plans is a daunting and formidable project. Perhaps that is because few of them have a framework to follow that guides them in shaping their plan. This section offers such a framework—a skeletal structure upon which a curriculum plan may be developed in which collaborative, active learning, combines with an emphasis on the development of higher-order thinking skills. It is not the only curriculum framework that is viable; others may be as useful. But this one, at least, offers a well-researched and successfully implemented structure upon which curriculum can be shaped.

It has already been described in other texts, for example, *The New Teaching Elementary Science: Who's Afraid of Spiders?* (Wassermann & Ivany, 1996); *Serious Players in the Primary Classroom* (Wassermann, 2000); and *Teaching for Thinking Today* (2009). The framework was not hatched in a university laboratory, but rather emerged from classroom teachers' creative efforts to design science curriculum experiences that promoted pupils' active engagement in scientific inquiries and the development of higher-order thinking skills.

It is described as Play-Debrief-Replay.

Play uses the well-documented idea that engaging in investigative play is an important way of building students' understanding of important concepts. Data from studies of children's play suggest that not only are conceptual understandings promoted, but also that this occurs much more substantially through play than through direct, systematic instruction. Play, moreover, invites and encourages creativity and invention, builds self-initiative, and provides for recurring practice of skills. It also involves students in hands-on and minds-on active engagement in the learning process.

For Play, the teacher designs an activity in which students work in small groups to carry out these focused investigations, which emerge from inquiries into the big ideas.

Debriefing follows the Play. It is a whole-class discussion in which students are called upon to dig more deeply into the various aspects of their investigations. In this Debriefing, the teacher attempts to promote analysis of the phenomena observed, stimulates conceptual awareness, promotes healthy skepticism, excites imagination, challenges ideas, and asks for data to support developing theories.

This is done by making it safe for every student to volunteer ideas without fear of rejection, by welcoming and appreciating students' contributions, by showing keen and genuine interest in their theories. Analyses are encouraged by asking questions, for example, "What are the supporting data?" and "Why do you suppose that it true?" and "How might you account for that?"

In the discussion, hypotheses emerge, discoveries are examined and explored. But no closure is brought and the inquiries are left "suspended" so that there is increased motivation for the students to continue their explorations in Replay.

During Debriefing, emphasis is on extracting meaning from the investigative Play. Chapter 7, "Developing Competence: Teacher-Student Interactions," provides information and practice tasks in promoting skill in using those higher-order responses and questions that enable the search for meaning.

Replay follows Debriefing, generally over the next days. Replay may involve repetition of the acts until skills are mastered; it may be a time when investigations are replicated and confirmed, or when new hypotheses are tested. New materials may be added that extend the investigations and broaden the learned concepts. This entire process is cyclical and terminates when the teacher or students implicitly or explicitly concur that certain materials have been sufficiently exploited. It is time then to "conclude" the work on this curriculum plan and devise a new one.

c. Knowing How: Creating a Curriculum Plan

What follows is an example of how one middle-grade teacher used the Play-Debrief-Replay framework to design her science curriculum plan.

She began by identifying her learning goals for the activity:

- *To promote understanding of the role of germs in disease*
- *To promote understanding that germs are living microorganisms that invade the body*

Then, she identified the big ideas from which the plan evolved:

- *Most diseases are caused by microbes that invade the body. A more familiar term for these microbes is* germs.
- *Germs can enter the body through the air we breathe; through eating food or drinking water; through breaks in the skin; or through the bite of a carrier.*
- *Understanding more about how germs are spread helps us to prevent the spread of disease.*

She described the thinking operations that were included in the activity: *Observing, suggesting hypotheses, examining assumptions, classifying, interpreting data, summarizing, creating, and inventing.*

Then, she designed the Play activity (gathering knowledge):

In the Play, students work in pairs or trios to gather knowledge about certain scientific phenomena. She has written directions on an activity card that the students use to guide them in their task:

> *Work with two partners and make a survey of everyone in the class who has had one or more of the following symptoms of illness in the last month: fever, sore throat, cough, sneezing, rash, vomiting, bellyache, or other illness that caused absence from school.*
>
> *Create a graph to show which classmates have had one or more of these symptoms of illness.*
>
> *Find out what these students did for their illnesses and working together write a summary of the different remedies they used to help them get well.*

Following the students' engagement with gathering data during the Play stage, the teacher then calls them together for a Debriefing. She has also prepared these few questions in advance that give her the "prompts" to keep her discussion on track.

- *What observations did you make about the different kinds of illnesses that have been going around in your classroom in the last month?*
- *What observations did you make about the illnesses that occurred more frequently?*
- *What observations did you make about the numbers of students in your class affected by those illnesses?*
- *What observations did you make about what students did to help themselves get well again?*

Sample Debriefing questions she might use that are more challenging and raise the level of thinking include:

- *How do you suppose people get colds? What are some hypotheses to explain it?*
- *Where do you suppose germs come from? What are your theories? What assumptions are you making?*
- *What do you know about different kinds of germs? Where do these ideas come from? What assumptions are you making?*
- *What do you know about how germs come into our bodies? What are your theories about it?*
- *How do people try to prevent catching a sickness caused by germs? What ideas do you have about that?*

- *What do you know about the kinds of illnesses that are caused by germs? How do you know that is true?*
- *How does washing hands help in the prevention of germs being passed from one to another? What are your theories about it?*

Of course, not all of these questions are used in a single Debriefing.

The time allocated to Debriefing will vary and depend on many factors, including students' interest, scheduling, and the teacher's perception of when to call a halt. In Debriefing, no issue is "resolved." Leaving issues unresolved is an important condition that leads to students' cognitive dissonance and hence further thinking and inquiry. It also provides impetus for the next stage: Replay.

Replay provides students with the opportunity to use the knowledge gathered and their understanding to take their inquiries further, and to apply what they know to practice. At this stage of their inquiries, the teacher has prepared several activities for the students continue their inquiries. During Replay, students continue to be actively engaged as they work in pairs or trios on activities that enable them to extend their thinking about germs.

Examples of Replay Activities:

- *Work with a partner. Use the library or the internet to gather information you need for this activity. Create a poster or a web page of your own design that describes four different kinds of germs: virus, bacterium, fungus, protozoa.*
- *Work with a partner. Create a poster or a web page that describes how your classmates can take precautions against spreading germs. Give your poster a catchy title.*
- *Work with two partners and use the internet or the library to find out what you can about diseases that are caused by germs. Write a summary of your findings.*
- *Work with a partner and use the library or the internet to find out what you can about these two scientists who played major roles in identifying germs as the cause of disease: Semmelweis and Lister. Working together, write a summary that describes the contributions of each of them.*
- *Work with two partners and use the library or the internet to find out what you can about the Black Plague. Working together, write a summary about the causes of this disease, how it spread, what happened to the people who got sick from it, and what was done to prevent the disease from spreading.*

Before the curriculum unit on germs is concluded, the students engage in some self-evaluative activities, reflecting on their work and their growing understanding of the role of germs in spreading disease. This may be done in a whole-class discussion, in teacher-student conferences, or in a written exercise. For example:

- *Tell about your growing understanding of the role of germs in spreading disease.*
- *Tell about your growing understanding of what germs are and what they do to make you sick.*
- *Tell about your growing understanding of how germs are spread and what we can do to prevent the spread of disease.*
- *Tell about how you used your growing understanding to carry out some of these activities.*
- *Tell about some of the challenges you faced in any of these activities.*
- *Tell about how you dealt with those challenges* (adapted from Wassermann, 2009).

DO IT YOURSELF

Using this framework Play-Debrief-Replay, the preservice student is now called upon to create a curriculum plan that might be used for a particular group of students, in a chosen school setting, at a particular grade level. If a student teaching placement won't provide the opportunity for students to develop and implement such a curriculum plan, the framework will, at least, provide novice teachers with the means and the understanding of doing this on their own.

NOTES

Classrooms today are veritable cauldrons of problems. In some districts there is visible evidence of systemic racism, economic hardship, generational poverty, crime, and violence. Students both younger and older present learning problems that are daunting. Some children live in fear of being deported by ICE because they are undocumented. More than a few live in single-parent households; more than a few have fallen behind in academic work because they have been out of school during the year of the COVID-19 pandemic. Some children are so pressured by parents to succeed that they live in high anxiety of failing parental expectations. In some districts, drugs are an ongoing problem; many urban schools now have metal detectors and security guards to protect children from lunatics with guns.

More than few secondary schools have special classes for 15- and 16-year-old mothers, with full-time day care provided for their babies within the school. The internet spreads disinformation that infects minds like a virulent disease. The fear of the spread of COVID-19, wearing masks, and getting vaccinated continue to be pressing issues of concern.

There's more. Many school-age children are sophisticated users of informational technology, with their own mobile phones, their own tablets, their own laptops. Many of them are what has been referred to as the "tablet generation." As one eight-year-old student told the visiting teacher who was introducing the iPad to his class, "I been doin' this stuff since I was three years old."

It doesn't take a wizard to appreciate the many and diverse challenges that teachers face as they do their utmost to bring knowledge and awareness to groups of often disinterested or "tuned out" children. Multiply that by the poor working conditions in many schools, the budgetary shortfalls, the sometimes irrational demands of administration and parents, what faces new (and experienced) teachers is formidable. The "tried and true" ways of instruction, in which students sit passively absorbing information, as teachers use "telling and showing" as their primary means of delivery of information, has been, for many years, considered ineffective. These days it is downright impotent.

While teachers cannot be expected to address all of the issues that are prevalent in contemporary classrooms, engaging students actively in the learning process is one way, arguably, not the only way, to advance their knowledge and understanding. Working in groups allows them to share ideas, to support each other, to learn to cooperate in their inquiries. Providing them with the tools to use to advance their knowledge is not a magic cure-all, but these ingredients go a long way to address more than a few of, but not all, the challenges teachers face.

Preparing preservice students to **know**, to **understand**, and to **know how** to build curriculum experiences that incorporate these features should be high on the list of what professors of education do as they prepare their students to face the new world of classroom teaching.

Chapter 9

Developing Competence
Student Teaching

Harry Evans was an assistant professor of education, with major in philosophy, who was assigned, as part of his teaching load, the supervision of student teachers. He came to his academic appointment directly from the completion of his PhD, absent of any teaching experience in the public schools. His student teaching assignment meant that he would get six credits toward a full teaching load, leaving him with the preparation for teaching only two on-campus courses. It also meant that he had more degrees of freedom with respect to time; he could visit student teachers at his convenience and spend as much time as he wished in those class visits.

He had, in fact, accepted this assignment because it seemed easier than preparing for and teaching four on-campus courses. It didn't matter that his own public school teaching experience was nonexistent; it didn't matter that he was unfamiliar with the curriculum standards, teaching strategies, the various problems and issues of contemporary education. In fact, none of these criteria were in consideration when he accepted the assignment.

To the administrative assistant to the dean, who was responsible for faculty assignments, it was sufficient that Evans was willing to accept the job of student teaching supervision. It was an assignment that academics normally thought beneath them.

STUDENT TEACHING SUPERVISION

Evans's first visit was to observe Phyllis Hansen. Her placement was in a third-grade class in a neighborhood where crime and other acts of violence were a daily threat in the lives of children and adults, where drugs were often openly traded on street corners, and where poverty was systemic, revealed in the nature of the broken-down houses, the uncollected garbage, the homeless sheltered in cardboard boxes on the street.

The doors of the school were locked and a security guard was stationed at the main entrance, checking for weapons. One had to pass through metal detectors before being permitted entry.

To add to existing problems in Phyllis's class, many children were new immigrants, with limited English; free lunch was their only hot meal of the day. For Harry Evans, whose own elementary and secondary school experiences were in the middle-class suburbs, what he saw on his first visit both shocked and alarmed him.

Evans had been given six student teachers to supervise, each placed in schools across the city. No attempt was made to assign schools according to their "educational value." Rather, they were chosen because they were willing to accept teachers-in-training.

Evans had phoned Phyllis Hansen and alerted her to his visit, so she knew he was scheduled to come. She had prepared a story that she would read to the class, and a list of questions she would ask them to check their comprehension. She described this as a "language arts lesson."

Evans nodded to her as he came into the room and introduced himself to the teacher, with whom he had a brief chat, and who said she would absent herself during the observation, so that Phyllis would have a chance to be on her own. Evans slipped into a seat at the back of the room, wedging his large frame into the small chair. He took out his tablet, ready to take notes about what he saw.

Some of the children looked back at him; none smiled and others ignored him. Phyllis called them to attention, told them the name of the story and a little of the narrative details. She then proceeded to read, standing at the front of the room. Two children began to talk to each other and Phyllis interrupted and scolded them. A few of them looked out of the window, showing their inattention. One girl in the back row had her head on the desk and appeared to be sleeping. Again, Phyllis stopped reading and reprimanded them for not listening. She had to interrupt the story several more times to ask children to pay attention. By the time she had finished reading, her anxiety was palpable, the children observably restless.

She put the book down and began to ask her questions. There were no responses; and she scolded the children for not paying attention and for their non-responses to her questions. Some of the children put their heads down on their desks. Not knowing what to do next, Phyllis put her list of questions down and said, "Well, since you were so disrespectful during the story and can't answer the questions, I think you need to spend the next ten minutes with your heads down on the desk as punishment."

Evans got up and went to the front of the room, told Phyllis that he thought she handled that well, and left for his next visit across the city. In his car, he took out his tablet and made some notes about Phyllis Hansen:

She has good classroom management. Her sponsor teacher says she is very willing to learn. The story she chose to read seemed okay for the grade level. Her discipline seemed appropriate to the children's inattention to the task.

* * * *

Put a cobbler into a room where he must create a perfect soufflé, and he would be understandably lost. Give a chef a violin and ask her to play a Bach prelude and fugue, and she would be beyond perplexed. Ask an auto mechanic to perform some ice-skating axels, and she would be up the creek. Unless, of course, any of these highly skilled people in their own fields had a second competence in cuisine, music, or ice skating. In other words, asking a person to perform competently in an area in which he or she had no reasonable skills to do the job would ensure an unsatisfactory outcome.

Yet assigning an academic to supervise a student teacher, without his or her having competence in supervision, understanding of the various professional tasks of teachers, curriculum standards, classroom management, and other related teaching tasks is a guarantee to breed incompetence in student teachers. With little or no professionally competent feedback emphasizing strengths and areas of needed growth, with no advice about what more needs to be done to improve competency, with an assessment that borders on the inane, there is very little chance that a student teacher will have an opportunity to grow and develop as a competent professional.

WHAT TO LOOK FOR IN THE SUPERVISION OF STUDENT TEACHERS

Poor Harry Evans. What he wanted most was to find a place for himself among his colleagues, to show himself as a worthy academic, to apply for and get grants to carry out research, to get tenure, promotion, and merit raises. Without any experience or expertise in the supervision of student teachers, he was at a total loss with respect to what to look for in assessing student competence. As a consequence, he focused on the "tried and true" issue of "classroom management"—for what was important in getting students to listen to what you had to teach them?

In chapter 2, the Profiles of Teaching Competency were described as one faculty of education's goal statements that presented nineteen competencies considered to be some of the most important tasks of classroom teachers. That evaluative instrument gave student teaching supervisors a basis for observing and evaluating student teaching competence. In other words, they knew what to look for and they understood how to make assessments that were based on focused observations of how well the student was performing at those tasks.

It takes a trained observer to perceive and recognize the various acts—both overt and subtle—that a teacher carries out during the course of a school day. There are non-obvious acts, as well as overt on-the-scene tasks that constitute "teaching." For example, before the day begins, teachers have in hand lesson plans that they have prepared in advance. They have a framework for the day's activities laid out. They may also have read and "marked" students' papers. They may have had telephone conferences with parents. All of these "behind the scenes" activities are integral to what a teacher does.

In their "on the scene" work, beyond the "instructing, showing how, demonstrating, and giving examples," teachers use "teacher-student interactions" that are specifically appropriate to certain learning conditions (e.g., those that attend to students' feelings, those that ask for information, those that extend students' higher-order thinking). Teachers also use observations of behavior that point to pupils' specific learning needs, diagnosing and responding to presenting learning problems. They continue to make informed, intelligent observations of student behaviors and they use those data to make diagnoses of problems that interfere with learning.

In classroom discussions, or talking to individual students, teachers use responses and questions that are carefully selected and appropriate to individual situations, using reflective responses and higher-order questions to encourage student thinking. Overall, they listen, attend, and apprehend what students are saying and they select, from a range of options, the types of responses to be made, with full appreciation that different responses have different effects.

Moreover, they are able to design curriculum experiences that engage students in "minds-on activities" rather than having them sit passively absorbing information. They understand that curriculum requires active engagement with the content. They allow students time to think.

These are some of the many and varied "tasks of teachers"—from inside of and outside the classroom. Without appreciation of those various acts, it is impossible to observe and understand the process of student teaching supervision.

If a faculty of education has failed to deliver a set of teaching competencies for supervisors of student teaching to use as guides in making their observations, they may, instead, find the Profiles of Teaching Competency (Wassermann & Eggert, 1994) helpful. The profiles have been described in chapter 2 and an entire copy may be found in the text *Mastering the Art of Teaching* (Wassermann, 2021).

Not to be neglected is the importance of involving the student teacher in the act of self-evaluation of his or her work. This, of course, is best done when the student teacher also has, in hand, a copy of the evaluative criteria on which the observation is based. One cannot evaluate in the absence of criteria; what results is either too specious or too general to be of use.

So every classroom observation of a student teacher should be followed by a conference, either one-on-one or including the classroom teacher as well, beginning with a request to the student for a self-assessment of how well he or she has fulfilled one or more of the tasks being addressed in that classroom observation.

Concluding the conference, the supervisor might also ask the student teacher to suggest which tasks and areas of competence he or she wants to focus during the next supervisory observation.

THE ROLE OF A FACULTY ASSOCIATE

There are more than a dozen good reasons to use trained personnel to supervise student teachers; they are obvious to anyone with a concern for the improvement of professional competence.

First and foremost, such a person would need to have firsthand knowledge and experience with the many complexities of contemporary public education as well as with those professional competencies that are part and parcel of what a teacher does. Second, such a person would need to be trained in the art of supervision. Yes, Virginia, learning to supervise student teachers is as much a learned skill as it is an art.

In some teacher education programs, selected practicing teachers are seconded to the faculty, for a two-year term, to assume the role of student teaching supervision. These "associates" apply, are interviewed and screened, and are appointed *pro tem*, joining the faculty in all aspects of university life, with special emphasis on the supervision of student teachers.

In the best situations, these "faculty associates" begin their terms with an introductory workshop in the art and skill of supervision. This would necessarily include becoming familiar with the faculty's goals for the program—since these goals are intimately connected to supervision. In other words, knowing what to look for first, what the faculty has deemed significant in terms of developing professional competence, gives the "associate" a heads-up that allows for a clearly defined focus on specific tasks and competencies.

Another essential feature of such an introductory workshop is an emphasis on interpersonal skills training—that is, how the "associate" uses effective interpersonal skills in giving evaluative feedback to the student teacher. Most of us in the profession know that evaluative feedback given with a sledgehammer can do more than destroy a student's confidence and commitment to grow on the job. We also know that when such evaluative feedback is given with thoughtfulness, respect, and concern for the student as well as for the skills, the likelihood of improvement is considerably greater.

A third feature in the development of supervision competence is learning how to involve student teachers in making self-assessments of their work. Such a skill, learned early on in student teachers' professional lives, gives them the means and the understanding of the importance of "reflection on practice" for their ongoing growth as teachers. To be able to see oneself clearly and without defensiveness is probably the single most important factor in a teacher's ability to continue to grow and learn on the job.

Knowledge of the program's goals, found in the goal statements of the faculty for developing teaching competence, facilitative interpersonal skills, and enabling students to make non-defensive self-assessments are three essential skills for student teaching supervision. Having firsthand knowledge and experience in the public school arena is a given.

To provide a student teacher with the best opportunities to develop competence, the first step is to ensure that those who do the supervision are well trained to do the job.

Why would practicing teachers choose to apply for a two-year leave of absence from their schools to assume the roles of supervision of student teachers? Those who have made such commitments have cited several payoffs. Not the least is a break from the overwhelming demands of classroom practice and a chance to play a role of consequence in the training of new cadres of teachers. But of equal importance is what many claim to be a two-year experience of professional development—an opportunity to enrich themselves by reading, teaching adults, mixing with permanent faculty, attending workshops, and learning as teaching.

Some schools of education use "teaching assistants," graduate students who are pursuing higher education degrees, to supervise student teachers. In such cases, their selection for these roles should be based on the criterion of prior classroom teaching experience, which would be followed by an introduction to the art and skill of supervision. TAs are usually not the best candidates for the job, because their primary interests, understandably, lie elsewhere. But where there is a shortfall of money for hiring better trained personnel, teaching assistants, well trained, can become a viable substitute.

CLASSROOM PLACEMENTS

The conditions that lead to successful on-the-job training for student teachers are many and varied; some of these have been described above. One additional singular condition is where the students are placed for their practicum assignments. While on the surface this may seem a matter of locating schools and classrooms that are not too distant a travel burden for the student, the truth is that it takes more than a requirement of proximity to ensure the placement offers the best chance for a student's professional development.

The bottom line is that placing student teachers in a classroom that is less than advantageous nearly always ensures that the student will come away with not only "wrong" ideas about teaching strategies, but perhaps even ideas that are counterproductive to student growth and learning. Even a well-trained supervisor of student teaching will be at loggerheads in assisting students in such an environment.

There is no quick solution to the problem of student placements. In the first instance, the principal of the school must be willing and eager to accept student teachers as part of his or her educational mission. Second, classroom teachers, who are perhaps the most-hard working and frequently stressed professionals, may be reluctant to add another professional task—the daily supervision and guidance of a student teacher—to their teaching loads. So finding willing and exceptional classroom teachers is more difficult than it sounds on paper.

Yet this is a challenge that needs to be addressed—for placing students in less than excellent fertile grounds for learning may result in later teaching practices that are less than adequate to meet the complex demands of today's classrooms.

There are no easy ways to get around this; but one is for schools and faculties of education to amass a cadre of excellent and obliging classroom teachers who become, in some adjunct way, a part of the faculty's ongoing operations. In some faculties, these teachers are referred to as "school associates"—and they are given not only adjunct status in the faculty but also are recompensed with either a stipend or tuition-free credits for their work. Moreover, they are invited to faculty occasions and honored for their work in the process of student teacher training.

These small ways of rewarding and honoring classroom teachers for the additional work they undertake go a long way toward their willingness to accept student teachers.

GRADING AND MARKING—
A DIFFERENT PERSPECTIVE

This chapter has advocated some new and innovative ideas for the supervision of student teachers. And if the reader has not been sufficiently put off by this time, another even more radical idea is being presented in this last section of the chapter. It suggests that as an alternative to using traditional grades for student teaching, students should be evaluated, instead, with Pass-Withdraw.

The section in chapter 4 on Grading and Marking offers some history of how the Pass-Withdraw grading system came into operation at the then new Professional Development Program at Simon Fraser University in 1966. It also describes the educational values behind such a change and the dynamics in the process of both the faculty and the university's acceptance of that change. Finally, it also gives evidence of the long-term effect of using Pass-Withdraw on the development of student teaching competence.

The rationale for such a change in grading makes clear that once in effect, students work to develop competence rather than working to get an A. And the history of that change is evidence that nothing has been lost in terms of the quality of the program and its design to promote excellence in teacher education.

Should other schools of education follow suit? It is not a critical or essential change—and not a lot is lost if traditional grading practices continue, and/or if a faculty does not want to assume the burden and take the hard knocks of raising such a proposal in the university senate. But should such a shift in practice be pursued and the battle for the change won, it speaks loud and clear about what the education faculty considers important and what they see as essential features of a program that has, as its priority, the preparation of excellent teachers.

NOTES

It has been said that there are no revolutionaries in the field of teacher education. And perhaps that is why reform has been slow to take; and that even effective reform movements that have ignited shortly died out in the absence of "fuel" to support them—"fuel" being those with the commitment to those ideas to sustain such innovation over the long haul.

Yet despite the deeply entrenched traditional teacher education programs that have persevered primarily by the fact that students are willing to come and enroll in what, to them, seems an easy road to a degree, there are bright lights across the universe of education faculties—places of inspiration and hope and enlightenment, where the emphasis is on educating and developing competent teachers. In this chapter, some radical ideas have been offered to point the way toward some more effective practices and changes that might be made.

In the end, when professors of education make choices, they will inevitably choose what's important. It is the hope of this writer that some of them will choose the development of competence for those students who want to enter this noble profession.

Chapter 10

In Retrospect

Becoming an academic meant, to me, being anointed as one of the favored few who were now presumed competent to take on leadership roles in the preparation of new teachers. In my initiation to the academy, I was given several courses to teach by the chair of the department, with no cognizance of my expertise to teach any of them. I joined the cadre of the professorial ranks and blindly found my way to teach Introduction to Education (which could have included anything), plus some "methods" courses, about which I had a bit of expertise, having spent a dozen years in the public schools.

My colleagues were sympathetic to my naivete and took pains to help me feel a part of the faculty. I spent four years at that teacher training institution, never questioning if what I was doing had any positive effect on what those being "trained" would do when they entered the profession. In retrospect, I compare that to "treading water"—no thought behind the actions other than seeing that students met the course requirements, a sort of "standing in place" with no forward movement.

Maybe some "seeds" were planted; maybe some of those beleaguered students found a way to use what I was advocating when they left the program and found their way into their own classrooms. It never entered my mind that "telling" students what they should do had little or no relationship to promoting their classroom expertise.

When I was "recruited" to take a professorship at the very new Simon Fraser University, to build a new teacher education program that was radical in its overall design, I had no idea of how to "fill in the blanks" of the program's design of three "preparatory" semesters of professional development. In my feeble attempts to put some structure into that loose framework, I reached out to learned colleagues at various colleges and universities and asked them about their ideas for what should be included in those three semesters. The results dumbfounded me; they knew as little as I did. All of their expertise in the academy consisted of "teaching courses"—much the same as mine.

One of the advantages of the very "loose" three-semester professional development program was its "looseness." Such flexibility allowed me to initiate plans, see how well they were working, and modify, sometimes in major ways, to compensate, to rectify, to improve what needed changing. And as a result of all of this on-the-job "field testing," those of us on the ground learned a lot more about what needed to be included in a teacher education program.

That long-term experience with the Professional Development Program at Simon Fraser University has been the basis for what has been written in this text. The ideas, strategies, and advice are offered humbly, because such efforts to change do not come easily. They require more than "ganas"—the desire. They require the courage to be different from the pack; to be innovative; to sometimes stand alone in defense of what one believes is right and good. They require the emotional strength to withstand the slings and arrows of those who tell you that what you are doing is bound to fail, and why should you even bother to try.

For those who are committed to making a difference, this book has offered what I hope are some concrete suggestions, ideas, strategies that have been used and have worked to create a huge teaching force that has, arguably, changed classroom teaching for the better in British Columbia elementary and secondary schools.

To sum up, then, here are some of the key principles that can be extracted from all of what has been proposed for rethinking teacher education that would lead to the promotion of more effective classroom teachers:

a. Be more selective in accepting students into the program. Be clear about the criteria being used in making those selections.
b. Include in the coursework the paradigm to know, to understand, and to know how. Ensure that coursework emphasizes not only theory, but classroom implementation.
c. Remember that "teaching as telling" in coursework translates into learning to teach by telling. Education students will not be "moved" to change their teaching strategies by listening to what they "should do."
d. Ensure that there is a means-end consistency between what is being done in the teacher education program and the goals of the program.
e. Appoint supervisors of student teaching who have firsthand classroom teaching experience and who know what to look for in assessing competence.
f. Be clear about the goals of the program, that is, about the essential competencies that are being promoted to achieve teaching excellence.

g. Create an ethos of caring for each student who wants to become a teacher; demonstrate in word and deed that their professional growth is of primary importance to you.
h. Make sure that all the coursework addresses what's important for pre-service students to know, to understand, and to be able to do.
i. Choose student teaching placements that offer the best, most highly prized venues for promoting a student teacher's understanding and expertise.

Will any of that work? Will such principles enable better preparation of those who want to enter the profession? As academics, we know enough to look at the evidence. Have those teachers who have graduated from our programs learned to teach effectively? Are we satisfied with our results?

Perhaps not every professor of education is ready to make a revolution in his or her academy. Perhaps no school of education is ready to turn what they do upside down and create a new framework, a new design, a whole new construct. Perhaps such a notion is too radical, even for those who would like to see change.

But change needn't come in a hurricane force. It may come in slow stages, piece by piece, at first, then gradually move to more grand designs. Perhaps it can begin with a small mini-program to serve as an exemplar of what is possible. Perhaps changes can first come within existing courses, that can more easily accommodate the know, understand, and know how framework.

In making changes that lead to greater professional competence, perhaps we can't do everything. But surely we can do more.

Appendix

CASE: I SO WANTED TO BE A GOOD TEACHER[1]

She passed by the school board office twice before she spotted the driveway that led into the parking area. Was it nervousness that prevented her from finding the road the first time? Or was she just a klutz, dressed up in a teacher's suit? She parked her little red VW, a relic from better days, in one of the visitors' spots, gathered her papers, and pulled herself up to the full height of her newly achieved status: *certified teacher*.

As she walked down the carpeted corridor of the administrative wing of the building to the door marked Personnel, she felt like a first grader approaching the fire-breathing dragon. The knot in her stomach tightened like a fist.

Dr. Alan Marshall, Director of Personnel, greeted her warmly. "Sit down, Miss Ziti. I'm very pleased that you could meet with me this morning."

The warmth of his greeting did little to dispel her anxiety, and when she tried to respond to his greeting, her voice came from a throat so dry the words felt like small dust motes that were blown into the air.

Alan Marshall's interview was brief. She had been told to expect complex questions on classroom management and teaching strategies, but his questions were so simple and direct that she could answer them with a minimum of sophisticated thinking. Yes, she had done her student teaching in a primary classroom, and yes, she felt she was ready to handle a class on her own. What else could she say? Certainly not the truth: "I'm terrified! I've never really handled a class for a long period on my own! I'm not sure of what a teacher has to do! I feel so—incompetent!"

As she searched his face for any sign that he might have picked up on her terror, her teacher training program, every moment of it, passed through her mind, as if she were drowning.

What were the important experiences? What had she actually learned about teaching? At this very moment, whatever it was she had learned had completely evaporated. She felt naked and incompetent. A fraud with a teaching certificate.

She must have said something right or else he must have been desperate for a new teacher. It was, after all, three weeks into the new school year. There was an opening at the River Road Elementary School, a primary classroom. The regular teacher has just left for maternity leave. She could begin on Monday.

"Yes, that's fine," she muttered, uncertain whether what she really wanted to do was run out of the office. She remembered thanking him for his time and for his confidence in her, and she remembered moving, like a zombie, past the desks of the secretaries and out to the safety of the parking lot.

"Whew! I've done it! I got the job! So what do I do now?"

She must have driven all the way home, because suddenly, she found herself pulling into space #63 in the underground parking garage that tunneled under the suburban high-rise. But she couldn't remember the drive, or the traffic, or even if she had stopped at the traffic light at the corner of Lonsdale and First Streets. Is this what anxiety did? Did it give you instant amnesia?

As Marilyn Ziti rode up the elevator to the ninth floor, she vowed to get a grip on herself. "This is ridiculous," she talked to herself in the mirror. "I've got to get it together here." She remembered what her mentor teacher had told her about nervousness during the first week of her practicum: Nobody dies from her first days of teaching! "Oh, yeah," she chuckled.

That evening she treated herself to a celebratory dinner of Caesar salad, spareribs, baked potato with lots of sour cream and butter, and apple pie, the $19.99 takeout special from Tony's Rib House down the block. Cholesterol City, right? What the heck. If you were sailing on the Titanic, you might as well go first class. But she vowed that the first thing Saturday morning she would take charge and get herself ready for Monday. Enough of these wild terrors. Nobody dies from their first day of teaching, right?

Armed with her second cup of coffee, the Saturday morning sun winking at the pile of papers, books, and laptop on the carpet surrounding her, she settled down for some serious planning. Like any good student preparing for a test, she read through her accumulated notes from her education classes. Here were all the answers she would need about teaching. In these notebooks, computer files, and textbooks lay all the secrets of the profession. If she could only remember them, she would have a clear line to a passing performance:

a. *Classroom management is one of the most important skills in effective teaching.*
b. *There are four definitions of creativity.*
c. *When you organize curriculum, you should not think of it as "set in stone" but rather as a guide in the teaching-learning process.*

d. *Educational objectives fall into three categories: (a) school objectives; (b) content or subject matter objectives; (c) teacher and child objectives.*
e. *Evaluation is the process of gathering data about student progress, both formally and informally, in order to further pupil learning.*

The ideas seemed familiar to her, but she took little comfort in the fact that she had once known them and been able to repeat them on tests to win high marks. What did any of them have to do with the reality of her, in front of 25 primary children, on Monday morning? She thrust the books, papers, and laptop aside and reached for the coffee.

With the most stressful weekend of her life behind her, she arrived at River Road School at 7:45 a.m.—early enough to meet the principal and walk on rubbery legs down the hall to her own classroom. There had been enough time to have her name put on the door, and she felt a thrill when she saw it—her room, her class, her children. The excitement of beginning to teach was running a close second to her anxiety. She wrote her name on the whiteboard, in large primary letters—MISS MARILYN ZITI—and sat down at the desk.

Helen Cameron, the teacher who had just gone out on maternity leave and had started with the class from the first days of the school year, had left detailed instructions for the new teacher. The class was three weeks into the fall term, and routines had already been established. As Marilyn looked at the teacher's plan, she saw how the reading groups were to be occupied, what seatwork was to be distributed, and what assignments were to be made in math. That about covered the morning until recess. When the bell rang at 9:00 she felt faint.

The children buzzed into the room, noisily and purposefully hanging up their outer garments, and proceeded to their seats. They sat quietly, peering at her. She swallowed hard, looking back at them.

"Good morning, boys and girls. I'm your new teacher, Miss Ziti. There's my name on the board. I hope we are going to have a very good year.

"It would help me to learn your names. So as I call your name, please stand up and let me see you. Let me know too if I am saying your name correctly." In retrospect, she thought that calling the names on the register was the best thing she did that morning. The children were quiet and she was in full control. After that, everything began to deteriorate. She tried to get the children into their groups, but a thousand small problems got in the way of her carrying out those simple procedures effectively. The more the operations broke down, the more disruptive behavior emerged. Pretty soon she found herself shouting.

"Sit down, Walter!"

"This is the last time I'm going to speak to you, Judy."

"No, you may *not* go to the washroom now."
"Why are you coloring when you haven't finished your work yet?"
"It's too noisy in here. Be quiet everyone."

The more she shouted, the more she felt she was losing it. She picked up the yardstick, in fury, and smacked it down on her desk. The children were startled and lapsed into silence. She hated what she had done and hated herself.

She somehow got through the rest of the day in a nightmare of tension and conflict. Her classroom felt like a battlefield, with a terrible power struggle going on in which she felt more and more the loss of control. She had the children get ready for home ten minutes before three o'clock and didn't care about dismissing them early. She hated every one of them and if she wasn't going to get fired for total incompetence, she would very likely resign. If this was what teaching was like, if now, after working so hard to complete her training program successfully, she still had so much to learn about teaching, she would be better off selling real estate.

STUDY QUESTIONS

1. What do you see as some of the important issues in this case?
2. What feelings does this case provoke in you?
3. Marilyn Ziti wanted to be a good teacher. What, in your view, is a "good teacher"?
4. What else might Ziti have done to prepare herself for her first day on the job?
5. What, in your opinion, got in the way of Ziti's effectiveness?
6. What would you advise Marilyn Ziti to do now?

NOTE

1. Reprinted by permission of the Publisher. Selma Wassermann, *Getting Down to Cases: Learning to Teach with Case Studies*. New York: Teachers College Press. Copyright © 1993 by Teachers College, Columbia University. All rights reserved.

Bibliography

Bracey, G. W. (1998). Minds of our own. *Phi Delta Kappan, 80*(4), 328–329.
Carkhuff, R. (1969). *Helping and human relations*. (Vol. 1). Holt, Rinehart and Winston.
Christensen, R. C. (1995). A community of learners. (Interview). *Harvard Gazette*. Harvard Graduate School of Business.
Combs, A. (1965). *The professional education of teachers*. Allyn & Bacon.
Combs, A., & Gonzales, D. (1993). *Helping relationships: Basic concepts for the helping professions*. (4th ed.). Allyn & Bacon.
Ewing, D. W. (1990). *Inside the Harvard Business School*. Random House.
Feynman, R. (1985). *Surely you're joking, Mr. Feynman!* W. W. Norton.
Freire, P. (1983). *Pedagogy of the oppressed*. Continuum.
Gage, N. L. (1966). Desirable behaviors of teachers. In M. D. Usdan & F. Bertolaet (Eds.). *Teachers for the disadvantaged*. Follett.
Greenberg, L. S., & Johnson, N. E. (1978, October). Towards a more authentic teacher. *Teacher Education*, 74–83.
Greenwood, G. E., & Parkay, F. W. (1989). *Case studies for teacher decision making*. Random House.
Henschke, J. A. (2013). From history to practice: How trust, empathy, reciprocity and sensitivity in relationships create the foundation of learning. *IACE Hall of Fame Repository*. Tennessee Research and Creative Exchange.
Kleinfeld, J. (1989). *Teaching cases in cross cultural education*. Cross Cultural Education series. University of Alaska, Center for Cross Cultural Studies.
Kowalski, T. J., Weaver, R. A., & Henson, K. T. (1990). *Case studies on teaching*. Longman.
Leland, J. (2016, February 28). Lesson learned: Dispelling myth of the hero teacher. *New York Times*, 27.
Levine, A. (2006). Educating school teachers. *The education schools project*. The Woodrow Wilson National Fellowship Foundation.
Lloyd-Jones, E. (Ed.). (1956). *Case studies in human relationships in secondary school*. Teachers College Press.
Moustakas, C. (1966). *The authentic teacher*. Howard A. Doyle.

Raths, L. E. (1964, May). What is a good teacher? *Childhood Education, XL*(9), 451–456.

Raths, L. E., Wassermann, S., Jonas, A., & Rothstein, A. (1986). *Teaching for thinking: Theory and applications.* Teachers College Press.

Rogers, C. (1961). *On becoming a person.* Houghton Mifflin.

Schon, D. (1983). *The reflective practitioner.* Basic Books.

Shapiro, B. (1994). *What children bring to light.* Teachers College Press.

Silverman, R, Welty, W. M., & Lyon, S. (1992). *Case studies for teacher problem solving.* McGraw-Hill.

Sparks, S. D. (2019). Why teacher-student relationships matter. *Education Week.* https://www.edweek.org/teaching-learning/why-teacher-student-relationships-matter/2019/03

Strauss, V. (2014, January 13). Is teacher education a disaster? *Washington Post.* https://www.washingtonpost.com/news/answer-sheet/wp/2014/01/13/is-teacher-education-really-a-disaster/

Truax, C., & Mitchell, K. M. (1971). Research on certain therapist interpersonal skills in relation to process and outcome. In A. E. Bergen & S. L. Garfield (Eds.). *Handbook of psychotherapy and behavior change: An empirical analysis*, pp. 299–344. John Wiley and Sons.

Wassermann, S. (1993). *Getting down to cases.* Teachers College Press.

Wassermann, S. (2000). *Serious players in the primary classroom* (2nd ed.). Teachers College Press.

Wassermann, S. (2009). *Teaching for thinking today: Theory, strategies and activities for the classroom.* Teachers College Press.

Wassermann, S. (2021). *Mastering the art of teaching.* Rowman & Littlefield.

Wassermann, S., & Eggert, W. (1976). Profiles of teaching competency: A way of looking at classroom teaching performance. *Canadian Journal of Education, 1*(1), 67–73.

Wassermann, S. & Eggert, W. (1994). *Profiles of teaching competency.* Simon Fraser University, Faculty of Education.

Wassermann, S., & Ivany, J. W. G. (1996). *The new teaching elementary science: Who's afraid of spiders?* Teachers College Press.

Zeichner, K. (2018). *The struggle for the soul of education.* Routledge.

Index

abuse, 46
acceptance, 29, 61–62
admissions: case studies on, 6–7; characteristics to consider during, 2–4; "gaming the system" and, 7; grade point averages and, 5; judgments and, 1, 5; portfolios for, 5–7; relationships and, 5, 6–7; to teacher education program, vii–viii, 1–7
ambiguity, 29–30
anxiety, 87–88
apprehending classroom discussions, 28
a priori strategies, 27
assessment: advice in designing tools for, 15–16; candidate "rating scale" in, 6; grading and marking, 37–38, 79–80; Pass-Withdraw grading system and, 80; for relationships, 5; student self-assessment, 23, 77; student teaching grading and, 37–38; of teacher education program, xiii–xvi; teaching competency and, 15–16
"attending," 28, 55–56, 60
authenticity, 2

behavior: student, 45–51; teacher, 11–15
"big ideas," 64–65

Cameron, Helen, 89
candidate "rating scale," 6
certainty, 29–30
change, xiv, 19, 83–85; innovation and, 4; radical teacher education program and, 33–39
characteristics: admissions and, 2–4; teacher behavior and, 11–12; in teaching competency, 11
children: abuse of, 46; growth and development of, 46–47; respect for, 2–3; troubled, 45–46, 49–51
Christensen, R. C., 28
classroom challenges, 45–46, 49–50, 70–71, 73–74
classroom discussions, 25–27; acceptance and being nonjudgmental in, 29, 61–62; conducting effective, 27–30; debriefing, 27, 60, 68–70; discussion teaching and, 28; examining issues rather than finding answers in, 29–30; listening, attending, and apprehending in, 28; role-play dialogues for, 60–62; teacher efficacy in, 27–30; teacher responses in, 53–57; teacher-student relationships and, 53–62; waiting for students to formulate thoughts in, 29
classroom immersion, 16–17, 33–35

classroom management, xiv, 23, 89–90; course design for, 24–25; student engagement and, 73–77; student teaching and, 21, 73–75
classroom observation, 17; from observation to analysis, 25–26; from observation to application, 26–27; reflection and, 24–28; student teaching and, 35–36, 73–77; theoretical framework and, 25–27
classroom placements, 73–74, 78–79
Combs, Arthur, 2, 9–12
competence. *See* teaching competency
competency-based performance index, 12–14
course design: for classroom management, 24–25; re-conceptualizing, 21–24
course planning, 9–10
COVID-19 pandemic, 47, 53–55, 71
curriculum: "big ideas" in, 64–65; creating curriculum plan, 67–70; essential elements in curriculum design, 64–70; higher-order thinking and, 66–67; innovation in, 4; knowing and understanding in, 64–70; play-debrief-replay and, 66–70; students and, 15; student teaching and, 76; teaching competency and, 63–71, 76; in triangular relationship, 13, 14–15

data, 25–26; in student teaching, 48–49
debriefing, 27, 60, 68–70
defensiveness, 3
dependency, 4
difficult situations, 45–46, 49–50, 70–71, 73–74
discussion. *See* classroom discussions
disinformation, 53–54, 71
dogmatism, 3–4

Eggert, W., 12–14, 76
Ellis, John F., 34
Evans, Harry, 73–75

faculty associates, 37, 77–78
Feynman, Richard, 35
flexibility, 84
Freire, P., 28

Gage, N. L., 11–12
genuineness, 2–3
Getting Down to Cases (Wassermann), 87–90, 90n1
goals, of teacher education, 9–12
"good teaching," 9–11, 87–90
grade point averages (GPAs), 5
grading and marking, 37–38, 79–80. *See also* assessment

Hansen, Phyllis, 73–75
Hicks, Carla, 24–26
higher-order thinking, 66–67
human relations, 34

immigration, 45, 74
innovation: change and, 4; in curriculum, 4; radical teacher education and, 33–38; in teacher education program, 9–10
interviews, vii–viii, 87–88
introductory workshops, 77–78
Ivany, J. W. G., 66

judgments: admissions and, 1, 5; avoiding, 39; nonjudgmental classroom discussions and, 29, 61–62; teaching competency and, 17

kid's kits, 48–50
knowledge: application of, 23; in curriculum design, 64–70; knowing, understanding, and, 19–21, 22, 57–60, 64–70; knowing how and, 20–21, 43–44, 47; learning and, 20, 22; teaching competency and, 43–44

leadership, 83; role models and, 13–14
learning and knowledge, 20, 22
Leland, J., 21

Levine, A., xiv
listening, 28, 55–56, 60

MacKinnon, Archie, 9, 33–34
Marshall, Alan, 87–88
Mastering the Art of Teaching (Wassermann), 76
meaning, 25
memorizing, 20
mnemonic devices, 20

The New Teaching Elementary Science (Wassermann & Ivany), 66

non-defensiveness, 3
non-dogmatism, 3–4

openness, 3–4

Pass-Withdraw grading system, 80
Paterson, Jack, 34
play-debrief-replay, 66–70
portfolios, 5–7
Professional Development Program, xv, 12–16, 33–38, 80, 83–84
profiles of teaching competency, 14–15, 76

radical teacher education: change and, 33–39; for grading and marking, 37–38; student teaching as, 33–38
Raths, L. E., 11, 66
re-conceptualizing course design, 21–24
reflection: on action, 22; classroom observation and, 24–28; by students, 23–24; theoretical framework and, 27–30
relationships: admissions and, 5, 6–7; assessment for, 5; human relationship attributes, 5; triangular, between teacher, curriculum, and student, 13, 14–15. *See also* teacher-student relationships
replay activities, 69

respect: for children, 2–3; in teacher-student relationships, 2–3, 54–55, 56–62
role models, 13–14
role-play dialogues, 60–62
Rose, Mike, 10
routines, 4
"self as instrument" concept, 12

self-assessment, 23, 77
Serious Players in the Primary Classroom (Wassermann), 66
shortcomings, 3
Simon Fraser University, 9; faculty associates at, 37; Professional Development Program at, xv, 12–16, 33–38, 80, 83–84
"specific competencies," 10–11
student behavior, 45–51
student engagement, 73–77
students: curriculum and, 15; reflection by, 23–24; responses by, 58–62; self-assessment by, 23, 77; teaching competency and, 45–51; waiting for thoughts of, 29. *See also* teacher-student relationships
student teaching: assessment, 37–38; classroom management and, 21, 73–75; classroom observation and, 35–36, 73–77; classroom placements and, 73–74, 78–79; curriculum and, 76; data in, 48–49; faculty associates and, 77–78; objections to beginning with, 34, 38; as radical teacher education, 33–38; rationale behind beginning with, 35–36; supervision, 36–37, 73–77; teaching competency and, 73–81
supervision, of student teachers, 36–37, 73–77
Surely You're Joking, Mr. Feynman! (Feynman), 35

TAs. *See* teaching assistants

teacher behavior: characteristics and, 11–12; teaching competency and, 13–15
teacher challenges, 45–50, 70–71
teacher education program: admissions to, vii–viii, 1–7; assessment of, xiii–xvi; change in, xiv; goals of, 9–12; innovation in, 9–10; missing elements in, ix; planning, 9–10; radical, 33–39; re-conceptualizing course design in, 21–24; teacher preparation and, 9–10; teaching competency and, 9–17; theoretical framework for, 19–31; training program, viii–ix. *See also specific topics*
teacher efficacy, 12; in classroom discussions, 27–30
teacher preparation, xiv; with classroom immersion, 16–17, 33–35; classroom observation and, 17; teacher education program and, 9–10; teams, 16–17, 36
teacher responses: "attending" and, 28, 55–56, 60; in classroom discussions, 53–57; student responses and, 58–62; study sheet for, 60–62; that are challenging, 56–57, 61–62; that ask students to reexamine ideas, 56; that call for analysis, 56; that diminish student thinking, 57, 61
teachers as role-models, 13–14
teacher-student relationships: authenticity and, 2; classroom discussions and, 53–62; importance of, 1; important characteristics in, 2–4; interactions and, 13, 15; knowing, understanding, and, 57–60; power of, 62; respect in, 2–3, 54–55, 56–62; role-play dialogues and, 60–62; teaching competency and, 53–62; in triangular relationship, 13, 14–15

teacher training, 12; introductory workshops and, 77–78. *See also student teaching*
teaching assistants (TAs), 36–37, 78
"teaching as telling," 63
teaching competency: assessment tools for, 15–16; characteristics in, 11; competency-based performance index, 12–14; curriculum and, 63–71, 76; developing competence, 43–51; "good teaching" and, 9–11, 87–90; judgments and, 17; knowledge and, 43–44; profiles of, 14–15, 76; "specific competencies," 10–11; strategies for promoting competence, 48–50; student behavior and, 45–51; student teaching and, 73–81; teacher as role-model and, 13–14; teacher behavior and, 13–15; teacher education and, 9–17; teacher-student relationships and, 53–62; triangular relationship and, 13, 14–15; what is important in, 45–47
"teaching for thinking" paradigm, 21–22
Teaching for Thinking Today (Raths et al.), 66
teaching incentives, xiv
teaching life, 16–17
teams, 16–17, 36
theoretical framework: classroom observation and, 25–27; knowing, understanding, and knowing how in, 19–21; putting framework into action, 24–25; re-conceptualizing course design and, 21–24; reflection and, 27–30; for teacher education program, 19–31
triangular relationship, 13, 14–15

understanding: in curriculum design, 64–70; knowledge, knowing, and, 19–21, 22, 57–60, 64–70; memorizing compared to, 20; promoting, 47; in teacher-student relationships, 57–60

Wassermann, Selma, 12–14; *Getting Down to Cases* by, 87–90, 90n1; *Mastering the Art of Teaching* by, 76; *The New Teaching Elementary Science* by, 66; *Serious Players in the Primary Classroom* by, 66

YouTube, 23

Zeichner, K., xiv
Ziti, Marilyn, 87–90

About the Author

Selma Wassermann has long and extensive experience with teacher education programs and is a founding member of the innovative Professional Development Program at Simon Fraser University. She is the author of more than twenty books and articles about teacher education, including *Mastering the Art of Teaching* (Rowman & Littlefield, 2021), *This Teaching Life* (Teachers College Press, 2004), and *Changing Course: Re-thinking Teacher Education Course Design* (Childhood Education, 2017).

www.ingramcontent.com/pod-product-compliance
Lightning Source LLC
Chambersburg PA
CBHW020126240426
43673CB00038B/611